Golden Rule
PARENTING

Golden Rule
PARENTING

Treat your child the way you would like to be treated

Gary M. Unruh, MSW

Lighthouse Love Productions, LLC
Colorado Springs, CO

Portions of this book are adapted and updated from the author's previous book, *Unleashing the Power of Parental Love*, copyright © 2010 by Gary Unruh, MSW.

First printing 2012
ISBN 978-0-9824204-0-9

CONTENTS

WEEK 1
"First, Please Understand Me"
How Your Child Wants to Be Treated (Part I)

WEEK 2
". . . And Help Me Become a Better Person"
How Your Child Wants to Be Treated (Part II)

WEEK 3
"Now, Help Me Treat Others as I Want to Be Treated"
Helping Your Child Treat Others with Love and Respect

ACKNOWLEDGMENTS

THE FINAL WORDS, PARAGRAPHS, chapters, and finally a finished book express the visual evidence of people who have profoundly influenced an author's life. Words cannot adequately convey the gratitude I have for these individuals who have made this book possible.

Without Mary McNeil, my chief editor, this book would not have been possible. A good editor combines straightforward feedback with a gentle attitude. That's you, Mary. Thank you for all your dedicated work.

Thank you, Dan Benson, for your editorial overview and your wise Christian input and invaluable suggestions for marketability. Your counsel strengthened my resolve to share my message.

Developing *Golden Rule Parenting* would not have been possible without the opportunity to counsel more than twenty-five hundred clients. I feel honored to have had the opportunity to help each of you to unleash your unlimited love for your children.

To my family I owe my inspiration to write this book. From my wife, Betty, I witnessed the miracle of love that she bestowed on our four children, and this same love continues to shine brightly as she grandparents our nine grandchildren. And to my four precious children—Laura, Eric, Christine, and Jason—what a joy to see your love radiate to others. Through you I was inspired to write the last section of the book about respect, compassion, and humility.

Thank you, Mom, Dad, my brothers—Ken, Phil, and Stan—and Aunt Betty for teaching me many lessons about how to love myself and others. As I wrote this book, I became more aware of the priceless contributions each of you has made to my life and to the message I have to share.

The Transforming Power of the Golden Rule

ADAM SCRUNCHES INTO THE corner of my office couch, his blond hair cascading over his eyes as he drops his head. Mom starts. "I still can't believe Adam's Facebook post. He broadcast to the whole world that I never show any understanding." Then she rivets her eyes to mine as she leans forward in her chair. "I can't imagine doing that to my parents when I was eleven. You talk about embarrassing."

Staring at the floor, Adam mumbles, "Every time I try talking to you about my school problems, you say 'Why don't you use just a little of your smarts.'" Turning to his mom, partially brushing his hair away from his eyes, he adds in a cracking voice, "All I want is for you to just hear me out." Tears start running down his cheeks.

Mom turns to me and, mimicking Adam, says, "Just hear me out." She gives me that riveting look again. "That's all I do, for Pete's sake. Can you fix this mess?"

This kind of "mess" is what I eventually hear from every parent and child, and the mud can fly for weeks. It's miserable. But there is a fix—and it's not consequences, timeouts, or lectures. The starting point is Adam's comment: *Just hear me out*. Being understood, and feeling understood, is a must—especially at the beginning of all problem solving. That's how everyone wants to be treated. But it rarely happens.

In helping hundreds of families, I have found that the ancient biblical wisdom of the Golden Rule is incredibly timeless; it's just as relevant and effective today as it was centuries ago. "Do to others as you would have them do to you" was given to us by Jesus Christ himself (Luke 6:31), and it really is the key to establishing life-essential relationships, whether at work, in the neighborhood, or in the family. And, as my client families can attest, it works wonders between parents and their troubled children.

Translated into modern language, the Golden Rule might read this way: *Treat others the way you would like to be treated.* Doing so with your child will lead you to the following principle: Seek first to understand your child's point of view and help him or her to feel understood. With this essential, often missing, foundation in place you will realize progress you've hardly dreamed of with the challenges of everyday parenting.

Messes do get fixed by following the Golden Rule. And even more importantly, your child will learn how to treat others by your example. Your child will be transformed into a responsible, respectful, resilient person.

Let's briefly establish some basics about how the Golden Rule fits in to parenting. Then, in the following chapters, I'll show you the specific transformational strategies. Here's the Golden Rule adapted to parenting: *Treat your child the way you would like to be treated, especially when conflicts occur.*

Now we're ready for you to ask the most important Golden Rule question: How would you like to be treated—now, as an adult—and how do you wish you had been treated when you were a child? Notice the emphasis is on *would you like*, not how you actually are or were treated. How most of us were treated as children didn't always receive a five-star rating. And wouldn't all of us like to be understood just a little better in our day-to-day lives? Take just a minute now and write down your answers—and don't be surprised if you feel some sadness.

Which way would you like to be treated in the following example?

"I can see it's really hard to keep within your seventy-five-dollar monthly lunch budget. What can I do to help?" The receiver feels empowered and understood, encouraged to be good.

"You are so careless with money. I don't think you'll ever be able to stay within budget." The receiver feels disheartened and misunderstood, discouraged and shut down.

It's a no-brainer. When you feel empowered and understood, you experience the down-deep acceptance of "who I am now, imperfections and all," and you are more motivated to improve and become "who I want to be." The pleasure part of your brain lights up, a little, and you feel hopeful.

Powerful stuff, this Golden Rule.

So that's the essential premise: Feeling understood and encouraged to be good is how your child wants to be treated at the most basic level. I've heard it over and over from every family member I've counseled.

By now you may be wondering if I'm just another bleeding-heart therapist giving the same old line: Just help your child express her feelings; never hold her feet to the fire or you'll damage her for life. That's *definitely* not the message here.

The Golden Rule parenting message is this: Disciplining with firm limits *is a must*, but don't forget to understand your child's normal frustration with discipline. That's how your child wants to be treated: "I want to learn good behavior, and please understand my feelings as I struggle to learn to do what's good for me." This book is full of everyday tips about how to discipline through understanding.

Here's your child's experience: *It really feels good that Mom and Dad understand me and seem to like me even when they're upset with me. It sure makes learning how to be good not so tough. And I really want to learn how to treat others the way my mom and dad have treated me.*

Feeling understood and encouraged to be good is transforming; it speaks to feelings, the heartbeat of life. That's how children want to be treated. Make the Golden Rule the center of your parenting, and before your eyes you'll see your child's specialness blossom. That's living to the fullest.

Now let's roll up our sleeves and make it happen for you and your child.

The Three-Week Transformation

DISCIPLINE AND PUNISHMENT. THAT'S how our society defines a parent's basic job description for raising a responsible, respectful child. It's the only 25/8 job in the world, and the stakes are really high.

If you don't get it just right, others are quick to point fingers, sigh, and say, "Too bad that child didn't have better parents." In the meantime, you worry and second-guess yourself: "Am I doing this right?" Or worse, "Have I ruined my child for life?" All too often you're left scratching your head, thinking, *There's got to be a better way.*

There is a better way. And it's not society's discipline-only approach that bombards parents every day from the many parenting books and almost-daily media coverage of the parenting approach *du jour.*

No, the better way is the Golden Rule parenting approach—treat your child the way you would like to be treated. This one-stop-shopping approach is the result of my counseling more than twenty-five hundred families during the past forty years. Time after time every parent makes one thing clear: Discipline alone just doesn't cut it. Discipline is essential, but it's just the tip of the iceberg.

Here's the problem in a nutshell. The most important parenting step is missing: starting with the innermost emotional needs of you and your child. When this essential step has been thoroughly addressed, then disciplining—the second step—works a lot better as you fit your favorite discipline approach to the needs of you and your child. This emotional-needs-first approach really makes sense when parents consider carefully the way they would like to be treated. Invariably meeting emotional needs emerges as a parent's top requirement.

In just three weeks, you'll learn all about putting together three basic Golden Rule parenting aspects: (1) how to fully understand your child; (2) disciplining in a way that fits both you and your child; and (3) teaching your child how to treat others well. It'll take three additional months of sticking with it to be really successful.

So, why does this approach work so well? It helps you fulfill the most important human need your child has: to be and feel valued and understood, especially during disciplining. With this need firmly met, your child can easily be taught to value and understand others. Can you imagine a better result of your hard work?

I can't wait for you to try this approach. Follow the tried and tested tips in the pages ahead and your child will establish two essential human beliefs: "I like myself a lot" and "It's really important to show understanding and kindness to others no matter how different they might be."

With these beliefs securely established—along with healthy, consistent discipline—you can count on your child becoming a responsible, respectful, resilient person. And at the end of the day, you can look in the mirror and say, "Job well done."

WEEK 1

"First, Please Understand Me"

How Your Child Wants to Be Treated (Part I)

CHAPTER 1: "I Need to Feel Understood"

CHAPTER 2: "Please Start with Where I Am"

CHAPTER 3: "Please Know that I Really Want to Be Good"

"I Need to Feel Understood"

MOM TOSSES AND TURNS in her bed like a little boat bobbing in a treacherous sea. She squints at the clock: two a.m. Her mind races. *I can't believe I got so mad at Jared. But failing his science test gives him an F this quarter. He'll never get it together. Still, I shouldn't have yelled. I can still hear those awful words: "You're so irresponsible! Will you ever learn?" He's drifting away from me. I hardly blame him for swearing at me and stomping out the door. I heard his tires squeal when he sped away. What if he gets into an accident? What if he gets hurt? What if . . . ? It will be all my fault.*

Can't believe I'm crying again. I didn't think I had any tears left . . . . May as well get up and read.

Mom slips out of bed and quietly makes her way to the door. Just as she steps into the hall, Dad breaks the dark silence. "I can't sleep either. Let's go talk in my study."

They pad downstairs and sit on the overstuffed chairs in the office. Dad begins. "Jill, you chewing out Jared like that was really way out of line."

Mom can't believe what she's hearing from the person she'd expected to support her. She stands up and shakes her head. "I don't need this, Allan," she says as she turns and walks to the kitchen.

Dad sighs. *I blew it again. I just don't know how to stop Jill from getting so mad. Doesn't seem to matter what I say. Besides, she's always accusing me of working too long and not having a relationship with Jared. That must be why he's got such a short fuse and why he doesn't show interest in anything except for that stupid band of his. A sixteen-year-old kid shouldn't need me that much. He should know I love him. I work hard to get him everything he wants, but it's never enough. My dad did the same thing as I'm doing, and I turned—*

The front door slams. Jared walks in and gives Mom a disgusted look. "Mom, quit crying. You're such a baby."

"How dare you talk to me that way!" Mom says as she runs back upstairs to the bedroom.

Dad makes his way into the living room, trying to be calm. "Jared, you know better than to be so disrespectful to your mom."

"Dad, shut up. You do it to Mom all the time. Where do you think I learned it from?" Jared storms off and slams his door.

Everything is quiet now—everything except the thought raging through both parents' minds: *What have we done wrong to be treated like this?*

Sadly, this scenario is not uncommon. I know; I've had the opportunity to visit up close and personal with twenty-five hundred struggling families, not a whole lot different from yours and mine, during the last forty years.

If you have firsthand experience with these types of interactions, my heart goes out to you. It hurts to feel powerless as a parent and to watch your children derail.

Perhaps you're feeling a bit discouraged at this point. Well, hold on. I've found the way to stay on track, and the solution is simple (though not always easy to practice): Children need to feel understood. Once they feel that you "get" them, they are so much more emotionally ready to work with you. All it takes is parents learning how to fully understand their child. Unfortunately, we're not born to understand others; it takes training—and training is what I'm offering you in this book. I'll do everything possible in the following pages to walk you through the process of learning to fully understand your child.

Once you've mastered this skill, you'll see what I've witnessed over and over again: All problems contain an element of gold, something of great value buried deep within. If you dig down far enough, underneath the dirt you'll always find a valuable, worthy child. When you mine and fully refine the good parts of your child, the problems begin to pale in significance compared to what they once were.

"Come on," I can hear some readers saying, "you sound just like every other bleeding-heart therapist." Perhaps, but my experience with thousands of parents proves the value of understanding your child. Finding the good in your child is satisfying for everyone.

Read on, use the tips and guidelines, and you can arrive at the same result.

How Understanding Works

Let's see how the understanding approach works from several sessions I had with Jared's family.

Jill called and filled me in on the scene that opened this chapter. I could tell she was at the end of her parenting rope. We set an appointment, and Jared's parents arrived right on time.

Mom and Dad sat on opposite ends of the couch and Dad opened the conversation. "Jared's really become difficult during the last couple of years. Every time we try to correct him he has to have the last word, and now he's really gotten mean to us and refuses to—"

Mom interrupted. "He never was like that as a kid. He was always pretty willful, but eventually he did what we asked him to do. And he always got As and Bs, a few Cs in eighth grade. It got really bad his freshman year, especially when he got to be friends with Adam. They formed a band, and everything went downhill from there. He argues, doesn't want to be around us, his grades are terrible . . ." Mom began to cry and couldn't continue.

Dad picked up the ball. "We try to be a good family. We take vacations we usually can't afford, he's got everything—even a nice used car. And we even recently took a parenting class. The ideas were great—you know, consequences, taking things away. . . ."

"Don't forget to tell him that you work seven days a week," Mom said.

Dad bristled. "All right, I admit I'm not at home with him enough, but you sure do like the money. Besides, let's not forget to tell Gary about your yelling."

I stepped in, hoping to avert an all-out battle between the parents. "It's already clear to me that you both love Jared a lot and that nothing's working—and that you both see where the other one can improve. I'll help both of you to improve, but for now tell me more about the problem and what you're doing that works or doesn't work." Jill and Allan put their boxing gloves on the floor and spent the rest of the session filling me in on more details.

Things went fairly well through Jared's middle school years. He always had good friends, participated in family events, and got A's and B's. He also had a lot of musical talent and played trumpet and piano. Life got tough when Jared started high school. That's when the family adopted Lilly; she was just nine months old when they got her from China.

Mom and Dad have had a decent marriage with the typical differences. But now Dad often mentions Mom's quick temper and her "drama," and Mom will eventually remind Dad about "working too much," not being a "feeling person," and "never wanting to spend time with me." Now the marriage is super stressed, and these problems are taking center stage.

These parents are really trying. But they're failing. We all know the feeling; it's heart wrenching. And it happens to all families somewhere along their parenting journey.

But it doesn't need to. When understanding each other becomes the family focus, you can expect to see significant positive change at home.

God's Word emphasizes this need for families to live together in understanding rather than selfish contention. In his first letter, the apostle Peter urged husbands to live with their wives in an understanding manner and to "treat them with respect . . . and as heirs with you of the gracious gift of life" (1 Peter 3:7). Isn't it reasonable to extend this same advice to parents in dealing with their children with understanding and respect? By doing so, we'll go a long way toward setting the stage for effective disciplinary correction.

But it begins with the commitment to understand.

Later that week I saw Jared. Here's what happened as he began to feel fully understood.

"How's your day going, Jared?"

He brushed his mid-length hair away from his eyes, and with a forced half-smile said, "I'd rather be with my friends, but I'm here."

"Don't blame you. Do you know what this is all about?"

In a mimicking singsong tone Jared responded. "Yeah, my dad says you're going to fix me." He couldn't resist making "air quotes" as he spoke. "Good luck. They've tried this before. But they're the ones that need to be fixed. Last time it was three against one. They'll never understand me." He settled back in the chair and looked out the window. "I've only got two years to go before I'm out of here." After a moment, he sat up straight and looked at me intently. "Did they tell you about my band?"

"No, tell me all about it."

His phone beeped.

"I give kids two times to text if it's done fast," I told him.

His eyes flashed surprise. He shot off a text in a few seconds.

Thinking about his band lit him up like a Christmas tree. "Yeah, last year me and my friends started a new band and called it 'Me/N/U Music Together.'"

He couldn't stop smiling as he told me all about his pride and joy.

Then I turned the conversation to what he wanted to talk about some more—what needed to be fixed about his parents.

"I can't believe how much attention they pay to my sister Lilly. She can't do anything wrong. And Mom's always saying I'm older and don't need as much attention when I tell her Lilly's a spoiled brat." His eyes teared up, and he looked me straight in the eye. "I really don't care anymore. I doubt if Mom loves me at all. I don't need her anyway. Maybe I'll quit high school and go on the road with my band. You wouldn't tell them that, would you?

"My dad is constantly saying I'll never amount to anything being a musician. I'm really good, but he never listens to my band. And his favorite thing? 'Don't expect us to give you the money we've saved for your college if you can't get into college.'"

Here's my take on Jared's story. Although Mom and Dad have really tried hard, Jared doesn't feel understood. Jared's angry. And he should be. The way he's handling it, well, that's a problem for sure—and we'll be sure to address that. But for Jared and his family to make any progress, he must first feel that his parents both want to understand him and that they do understand him. This is where parent-child relationships most often derail—and where they stay derailed—until parents address this most basic need in the heart of a troubled child.

Here are the top three things, in Jared's words, Mom and Dad don't understand:

- "I love music better than school, and they'll never get me to choose school over music."

- "Mom loves Lilly more than me, and I doubt if Mom loves me at all." (Tears in Jared's eyes prove how much this hurts.)

- "Dad doesn't admire me and I don't care." (He really wants his dad to admire him—all kids do even if they act like they don't. It's easier to not care than to feel the hurt. Jared's pushed it all into the unconscious cave.)

Hey, Kids!

Kids, here's something to think about: You are not bad because you are messing up. Okay, when you say or do mean things, you're not improving the situation. But here's the deal. Some pretty mean stuff gets said when we're sad or mad. And your folks may not know how to fix it. Talk to an adult, counselor, pastor—someone like that— about your situation. They'll suggest ways to deal with your feelings without the mean behavior. Your parents will probably go along with it.

Jared's basically a good kid. Things were really decent until Lilly came into the home. Everything went south from there. When you add in his stubborn streak, you've got a kid who's dug in pretty deep.

But this situation is far from hopeless. He has some awareness of how much he wants to be loved by his mom and dad. He said, "I doubt if Mom loves me at all." The deep-down translation: "I really want my mom to love me, and I miss her love since Lilly came." And his feelings about dad: "He never listens to my band." Translation: "I really want my dad to admire me."

That's the slight twinkle of the good stuff (unrefined but still there) that's not visible because of all the dirt flying everywhere. It's all about being fully understood. When I showed interest in his band—his passion—his anger began to drain away. And, allowing him to text went a long way toward Jared's feeling understood. As he felt understood by me, his heart opened up and the hurt flowed out. That's the result of understanding—and you can do the same thing.

This fully understanding a child (or teenager or adult) stuff looks great on paper, but how does it really work? Let's take a peek into my counseling sessions in the next chapter with Jared's family and you'll get a good idea.

CHAPTER 2

"Please Start Where I Am"

DOES JARED'S SITUATION SOUND hopeless? Jared's convinced: "They'll never change." And Dad's given up: "I work hard to get him everything he wants, but it's *never* enough."

All too often we get stuck in a negative spiral of frustration and failure. You know how it goes; we do a lot of finger pointing and say "you never" and "you always" more than we want to. No matter how much we love our children or how hard we try, we hit a dead end. The situation is on our minds when we go to bed and pops up right away when we wake up. But hold on! Your relationship with your child doesn't have to unfold like that. There's hope!

It's all outlined in 3D living color in the next paragraphs. Read on and you'll find some help and encouragement for avoiding the seemingly inevitable hopeless times we all face.

First, you need to know the solution is simple—but not easy. Here it is: Parents need to replace their unsuccessful "my way or the highway" position with the effective "listening and responding" approach. It's all about paying attention to what's going on down deep inside your child—feelings.

Simply put, shift your focus from *you* to *your child's feelings* from the get-go. When you do, your child will feel understood and encouraged, and the Golden Rule will do its work: You'll be treating your child the way you would like to be treated—the way *everyone* wants to be treated. That's what it means to "start where I am."

And I believe it's what the apostle Paul was saying when he addressed dads (actually, all parents) on this very subject. "Fathers," he wrote, "do not embitter your children, or they will become discouraged" (Colossians 3:21). Paul was *not* saying parents should not discipline their children. Rather, he was reminding parents everywhere that there is a right way and a wrong way to deal with our children as they test the boundaries—and the right way is to treat our kids the way we ourselves would like to be treated. To *first listen and understand*, regardless of whether we agree with what they're saying.

Jumping to judgment and punishment without first listening and understanding only "embitters" (or exasperates) a child and inevitably causes him to "become discouraged" as Jared did. Effective correction starts where your child is, when you *seek first to understand* through listening before you seek to be understood. You're not necessarily agreeing with your child, but you're respecting your child enough to discipline him without disheartening and embittering him.

In just a moment you'll see how this all works, but first let's identify two really important requirements (one of them was just mentioned) you'll see throughout the upcoming session with Jared's family and the rest of the book. And don't feel bad if you're not doing these things; none of the parents I've counseled knew how to *consistently* practice these principles before they started counseling.

First, *start where your child is, not where you are.*

And second, *demonstrate that you want to and do understand your child's concerns.* Here's how your child needs to be treated by you when you consistently apply these principles: (1) he needs you to acknowledge that you've heard his point and (2) she needs you to support her feelings (not the behavior caused by feelings). Think *child's concerns first, discipline second.* (Discipline's covered in chapter 4.)

Let's stop a minute in case you're feeling what a lot of parents feel about these points: *This is sounding like permissive parenting* (where you don't ruffle a child's feathers for fear of psyche damage). *After all, children need to respect authority and do things whether they like them or not.* I hear you, and I'll double ditto that point. Permissive parenting does *not* work!

Your point about children needing to respect others and do what they're supposed to do is one of the most important end results of applying the Golden Rule.

But with the Golden Rule you don't start with what your child is doing wrong. You start with your child's feelings—what's going on deep inside your child. Only then do you move to problem solving. When they're treated this way, children always say something like this to me: "When Mom and Dad understand my thoughts and feelings first, I feel a lot more like being good."

Short and sweet: Inside feelings first, outside behavior second; and put your point of view aside (temporarily).

Hey, Kids!

Kids, there are some things you need to do as I'm helping your mom and dad understand you better. Blaming parents for everything is a big-time problem for almost all kids. I hear a lot of "If they would just stop yelling" or "They never understand me." Guess why they're yelling? I know, you're probably thinking, *They're just yellers. That's how they talk to me most of the time.* But more likely, the yelling usually has something to do with your behavior—like you're not doing what you're supposed to do. Instead of complaining about the yelling, try doing what you're supposed to do. Most of you will notice a lot less yelling. If they're still yelling a lot, ask them kindly to stop. Most parents will improve a lot. If that doesn't work, talk with your school counselor or pastor about what to do next.

With that background, we're now ready for the family session, beginning with Jared's mom and dad.

The first order of business is to help Jared's parents get their ducks in a row before we bring Jared into the situation. They need to find out how to shovel all the dirt aside (theirs and Jared's), ignore it for the moment, and find the deep-down cause of the problem. (You already know what it is, don't you?) They need to begin to pay attention to Jared's feelings, and then they must show understanding—a lot of it. That's a pretty big flock of ducks to line up just right, especially when you've not done it very often.

Mom opens up our time with a question: "I know this session's supposed to be about Jared, but can you help Allan and me not fight so much over how we parent?"

I smile. "Great idea. I'll teach you the same communication approach that I'm going to help you use with Jared.

"First, I want both of you to tell me one thing that bothers you about your spouse. The end goal is to fully understand each other. We'll need some rules and I'll be the referee, because our natural tendency is to defend our point of view the way football players defend their goal line. The closer the other person gets to 'scoring' (being 'right'), the more entrenched we become with our point. That negative spiral can grow into a tornado really fast, and once it does you usually don't have time to find shelter.

"That's not the Golden Rule approach. You don't defend your point by making the other person wrong. It's just the opposite. You put your points aside, which is really hard to do at first, by fully acknowledging and supporting the other person's *starting* points of view. With the Golden Rule, we win when the other person feels understood because it's at the heart of how people want to be treated."

This crucial point is underscored for us in Philippians 2:3¬-4, where the apostle Paul wrote about maintaining a Christlike attitude in all relationships––including (especially) our all-important relationships with our children. I've sprinkled this passage with a few bracketed amplifications to help us apply what the apostle was saying:

Do nothing from selfish ambition or vain conceit [like wanting to make our disciplinary point without first listening to and acknowledging our child's perspective], but in humility [free of personal pride; valuing the child's personhood, self-regard and feelings] consider others better than yourselves [remembering that this child is precious in God sight]. Each of you should look not only to your own interests [like getting a quick "win" at the risk of a longer-term loss], but also to the interests of others [remembering that it's vital for a child to feel *I'm valued; I'm okay* even in the midst of disciplinary correction].

"Here's the first rule to help us not defend: Listen while the other person talks—no buts." I pick up a clipboard and toss it onto the floor just out of my reach as I explain, "You've seen football coaches referring to their clipboards to show players the best defensive moves. That illustrates the way humans naturally behave until they use the Golden Rule clipboard."

I look at the clipboard on the floor and conclude, "Keep your defensive clipboard out of reach and you'll quickly get good at listening instead of defending."

Allan chimes in, "Yeah, now that I think about it, I'm constantly referring to my defensive clipboard, as you put it. And when Jill asks me if I heard her, I always say yes, but really I'm just making some mental last-second defensive adjustments. This is sounding pretty hard."

Jill's smiling and nodding like a bobble-head doll. I'm glad Allan doesn't see her expression.

Now, let's take a brief timeout from Allan and Jill and reflect on our own defensiveness. We all have it within us. Defending ourselves when we're challenged is just human nature. "I'm right" tends to be our immediate impulse on really important matters (even therapists struggle with this). The hope, at least for me, is that we'll catch ourselves when "I'm right" pops up, stop defending, and start listening. You may have already mastered this, but for most of us it's a work in progress.

It's a skill Jared's parents are ready to try, too, so let's get back to my response to Allan's comment about how hard it is to not be defensive.

"Allan, you're right on it. Pushing your point first is a sure way to kill understanding. We need a way to start with the other person so they feel understood right away. As you might guess, I just happen to have a useful tool that can help us do that. It's called the Discussion Procedure, and this approach to understanding has two stages: (1) concerns and (2) solutions (mutually agreeable).

"We'll start right away with the concerns stage and get to the solutions stage in our next session. The concerns stage includes two elements: (a) *listening to and repeating* what the other person says with no buts and (b) *agreeing with* and *validating* in some way the other person's feelings and thoughts. The great thing about this concerns stage is that you kill—I mean put to sleep temporarily—three birds with one stone. You successfully reduce defensiveness, the other person doesn't feel shut down, and you're not stuck with someone else's unworkable solution. "So, who wants to start with their concerns?"

Jill raises her hand as she looks at Allan. Allan nods and Jill begins. "Allan is gone so much he hardly spends any time with Jared. His new job started at the same time Lilly came to live with us." Allan squirms but doesn't make a sound. *Good job, Allan. Keep the listening channel open and push your defensive clipboard a little farther away.*

Jill continues. "Jared used to say he wanted his dad to be home more so they could do things together, but in the last year he stopped saying that. Now Jared's a lot more angry."

I look encouragingly toward Allan. "Allan, thanks for not saying anything. You managed the listening part really well. Are you ready for the first part of understanding—repeating what you heard Jill say? And remember, no buts. You'll get your chance to be understood on this issue after you show understanding to Jill."

Allan nods cautiously, looks at Jill, and successfully repeats everything Jill said. Then he asks her, "Did I get it?"

Jill darts a smiling glance at me and then at Allan. "Yes, you did." She looks at me with tears glittering in her eyes and says, "I can't remember being heard like that for a long time."

Allan frowns, starts to form a word, then stops.

"Great, Allan. You successfully completed part one of the concerns stage. She feels you listened to her and heard her; she knows your eardrums are working.

"Now we're ready for part two: *agreement* and *validation*. This part is about agreeing with something Jill said so she'll feel you really get what she feels; it's the heart part. As you can sense, Allan, this is both the hardest and most important part of achieving understanding."

Allan grimaces as he forces a smile, shakes his head slightly in agreement, and takes a cleansing breath.

Push pause for just a second. Do you get agreement right away from your loved one in your WWIII battles? Probably not. Would you really like it? Are bluebirds blue? Do we need it? Yes, yes, yes! Getting agreement is about as basic as breathing when it comes to feeling understood. I think we're all in agreement. Feels good, doesn't it? Let's get back to my instructions to Allan about this agreement part.

"Allan, just a few more points before you answer. Agreeing with a part or all of what Jill says doesn't mean you're waving a white flag. You're not saying, "You're right, I'm wrong, I give up." It just means you're in the early stages of problem solving, where each person needs to be treated with understanding. We're not yet at the stage of finding a solution. Want to give it a try?"

Allan nods slightly, squirms to find the most comfortable spot, turns to Jill, and says, "I agree that I work way too many hours, and . . . I agree Jared wants to be with me more." He looks at me, teeth clenched. "I'd love to say, uh . . . okay, I can't." He repositions himself again and looks at Jill. "I really can see how you would be so concerned." He looks at me, breathing like he's just finished lifting a hundred-pound cement sack. "That's the best I can do."

"Allan, A-plus. You did great."

I turn to Jill as Allan hands her the tissue box. "How are you feeling?"

She glances lovingly at Allan, wipes the tears rolling off her checks, and says, "That's the most loving thing I've heard for a long time. I think there's a chance this stuff will work." She reaches out to Allan. Their eyes meet, smiles cross both faces, and they hold hands, tightly.

Are you thinking this is too good to be true? I've witnessed this scenario time after time in my office. One spouse almost always tears up, and it's not unusual to see the two of them holding hands, though not usually this soon. What always happens is that hearts are touched right away to some noticeable degree. Why? You know what I'm going to say: The need to be treated with understanding during a problem seldom happens, but when it does, hearts are moved and great things happen. Can't wait for you to see this happen in your family.

Now, back to our session, and it's Allan's turn to be understood. We'll condense a bit, and I'll summarize. Allan talked about why he works so hard and Jill listened. She interrupted a little bit but self-corrected. Jill agreed with his reasons for working long hours and let him know how much she appreciated his hard work and how difficult it must be to seriously consider reducing his work hours. Allan felt understood.

In the next session the parents dealt with Jill's yelling. They worked out solutions for reducing the yelling and for Dad spending more time with Jared. (You'll learn the specifics about how to accomplish mutually agreeable solutions in chapter 6: "I Need for Us to Agree to Disagree Agreeably.")

Hey, Kids!

Kids, did you know that adults really struggle to understand each other when a problem comes up? That's why you see your parents arguing sometimes. They're busy trying to prove the other person's wrong instead of listening to and understanding each other first. Everyone acts like this, including you, but it's really not an okay way to solve a problem. That's all going to change by the time your parents finish reading this book. Your whole family will learn how to understand each other more, and you'll get along a lot better with your teachers and friends.

Parents, I'm hoping this understanding approach doesn't sound too good to be true. Even though it may sound a little fairy-tale-like, it's not. I think it seems that way because we defend so automatically. Because we do, we think defending is the only way to approach a problem. Of course, we all want to be understood—it would feel so good—but most of us have given up even hoping it'll ever happen. But I assure you, it will happen with the Golden Rule approach.

I've seen it over and over again *in just one session*: the Discussion Procedure stops the defending and starts the understanding. Why? You're starting where the other person is, not where you are. And because it's so rewarding, people really work hard to experience it again and again.

In just a minute we'll see how Jared's parents applied this understanding approach to their relationship with him. But first, I want to encourage you to start this approach right away with your loved one. It'll make a big difference in all of your relationships and really help when you test the Discussion Procedure with your child.

Here are some quick summary tips to keep in mind as you're test driving this approach.

- Push your defensive-play clipboard aside, farther than arm's length.

- Don't think about whether you're right or wrong during the concerns stage. Remember, you're starting with the other person, not yourself. For the moment, the person you're listening to is right because it's what he or she feels. (Later comes the solution stage, where the problem is solved and both your concerns are included. That's when you'll both feel right, finally.)

- Put yourself inside the heart of the one who's talking as if you are that person. Feel what they feel; it's the lifeblood of feeling understood. "I can see you're really upset; that's got to be hard." Remember the two essential inside-the-heart requirements: listening and agreeing.

- Write down the two parts of the concerns stage: (1) *listen to and repeat* what the other person says with no buts and (2) *agree with* and *validate* in some way the other person's feelings and thoughts. Short form: listen and agree. Have this page in front of you before you make your first attempt. If one person gets too upset, stop and start over later. Some things may require a counselor's assistance.

Now when a problem comes up, you're prepared to give the approach a try.

Let's get back to Jared's family sessions. Sit back, relax a bit, and I think you'll find some more useful tips.

Jared came in alone for the next session so I could show him the ropes about how the understanding approach works. At the end of the session he was not very hopeful but agreed to try. "I can't see how they'd ever understand me, but I don't have anything to lose."

The next week Mom, Dad, and Jared came in for the long-awaited family session. Dad came in first and gently asked Jared to sit between him and Mom on the couch. Jared tilted his head and said as he chomped on a big wad of gum, "Don't think so." He took the chair farthest away from them, turned his head, and stared out the window.

Jared had decided in our previous session that he wanted to share his frustration about how his dad puts down his band. So I start by looking at Jared and saying, "I've been helping your mom and dad to listen better. Do you want to tell them about your feelings related to your band?"

You could have heard a pin drop, even though my office is carpeted. A fast glance at Mom and Dad reveals statue-like people. I can hardly tell if they're breathing. To my surprise Jared seems the most relaxed as he breaks his gaze from the window and tilts his head toward his dad. "Yeah, Dad, what's up with your 'you'll never make anything out of yourself playing drums'? I'm kinda tired of that sh—"

I gently interrupt to set some rules. "Jared, I forgot to say that we need to do everything possible to say what we feel without swearing. I know you're really mad, but I'd like to see if we can deal with feelings without using bad language. What do you think?"

"Yeah, but I'm really p— uh, I mean ticked off." He swallows hard while he nods. "That's fair enough . . . I guess."

I turn to Dad. "Do you remember the understanding rules—repeat, agree, and no buts?

"I do, and I'm ready," he says with a welcome easiness.

I look at Jared. "Tell him how you feel about what he says."

Jared shifts his eyes away from me, leans forward in his chair, and says angrily, "I'm really PO-ed." He looks at me questioningly and I say, "That's acceptable."

He continues. "I don't care whether you think I'll make money or not. I love playing drums. It's the only thing that makes me happy. You guys sure don't. And I want you to stop putting me down." He shoots me a questioning 'did I do it right' look, and I give him a quick nod.

Dad squirms in his seat and Mom reaches out to touch his knee. Now Dad looks at me, I nod, and he looks at Jared. "I hear you saying the comments I've made to you are putdowns. And that your band makes you happy and that we don't make you happy and that you . . . you, uh, feel put down."

Dad looks at me and says, "What do I say now? I'd really like to tell him why I say those things."

"Allan, you did a good job. You can tell him your concerns later, but now you need to ask, 'Did I get what you said?'"

Out of the corner of my eye I can see Jared trying to hide his surprise. His eyes dart from me to Dad, waiting for the next comment.

Dad fills the loud silence, saying, "Did I get what you said?"

Jared looks surprised and stutters, "Yeah ... uh, yeah, you did." He looks at me and back at Dad. "For once, yeah, you got it, dude."

Then Dad looks at me. "Now's the agreement part, right?"

I was so glad we'd taken the time to practice this approach with Dad and Mom. Allan was flying!

Jared sits up straight in his seat and leans toward his dad. Mom's asking for the tissue box.

Dad says, "I, uh . . . I have made those comments, and they, uh, they're not right to . . . to say to anyone—let alone a son that I love a lot, especially when it comes to how much you love drumming." His voice cracks and he coughs to keep the water in his eyes from spilling down his cheeks. He looks square into Jared's eyes and says, "I'm going to stop saying stuff like that. It's not right." He bows his head. Dad seems to be catching on to the extended principle of 1 Peter 3:7; he's showing his son understanding and honor as a fellow heir of God's grace.

I look at Jared, who can't hide anything anymore and has that deer-in-the-headlights look. I ask, "How did you feel about your dad's comments?"

Jared shakes his head and says, "It's been a long time comin'." Then he squints first at Dad and then at me. With doubt in his voice he says, "I don't think he can do it outside this office."

Dad's still got his head down, and Mom's resting her hand on his knee.

When Jared makes eye contact with me, I gently say to him, "You're right, Jared, to *think* that Dad can't keep his word. There's not been much trust between the two of you for the last couple of years. But I know your dad a little bit and I know he really wants to make his relationship with you better. Do you think you can give him a chance?"

Dad looks up with the saddest expression I've seen for a while, waiting to hear Jared's response. Jared looks at me and then rivets his eyes on Dad. "Yeah, Dad." Jared throws me a quick sideways glance, licks his lips, and with a slight nod at his dad says, "Yeah, Dad, I'll give ya a chance."

Whew! How's that for openers? I don't know about you, but for me combining the tension of wondering which way this encounter might go with the exhilaration of a dad and a son touching each other's hearts so deeply made for one white-knuckle ride.

That's the radiant power of the Golden Rule: Jared desperately needed to be treated with understanding, and Dad pulled it off. Dad sidestepped his defensiveness, ignored Jared's negative comments, and admitted being wrong. Raise your fist high, Dad. You richly deserve your gold medal.

And not too shabby a performance by Jared, either. He's just like every other child: Being understood breaks down the biggest walls, and deep emotional connection is eventually the result.

Does this happen every time? Yes, eventually. One session will get the ball rolling if the problem of misunderstanding has gone on for only weeks. More sessions are required if it's continued for months or years. In Jared's case, the marital work his parents did made a big difference in helping Dad pull off what he did. When you combine Dad's rapidly developing understanding skill with Jared's needing to be treated with understanding, you get exactly what's needed for record-breaking close attachment to begin. Again, it didn't happen overnight. This family came in for a few more sessions to perfect their skills, but then they were ready to fly on their own.

And here's some really good news: Most of you can do this at home without a counselor or therapist. If the problem is too entrenched, however, don't hesitate to use the services of a professional to get the ball rolling in the right direction.

Hey, Kids!

Kids, just a quick comment before I give some last-minute encouragement to your parents. You should be frustrated when your parents don't understand you. But make sure you're not mixing up understanding with not getting your way. You know, when Mom says you can't wear shorts to school when the temp is thirty-three degrees. You feel misunderstood because you know wearing shorts would be great. But really, you're not being misunderstood; you're just not getting your way. Disappointing, but not the end of the world. Trust your parents' experience and accept their authority when you need to. Here's a tip to follow that will make life at home a whole lot easier for everyone: Give your opinion nicely, but follow your parents' final request. And about their understanding you? Expect a lot more of that after they finish reading this book.

Parents, I hope you've got a good idea about what it means to "start where I am" and the amazing benefits that come from starting from deep down inside your child's heart. When you first begin, expect some hefty bumps in the road (make sure your cheat sheet is in front of you to minimize the damage). But after several attempts, you'll get the hang of it and can expect to get the same results as Jared's family achieved.

I can't wait to get into the next chapter with you. Did you know that even when children are being bad or mean, down deep inside they want to be good? I know this is hard to believe when eight-year-old Michael is always putting down his sister or tween Emily wants to argue about everything. Find out for yourself in the next chapter what happens when you shift your focus from the not-so-good behavior to the deeper good within your child. It's another parenting gem from the Golden Rule.

CHAPTER 3

"Please Know that I Really Want to Be Good"

JEREMY'S VOICE CRACKS AND his cheeks glisten with tears. "Every trip home from hockey games Dad yells at me about what I did wrong. I'm trying hard, but Dad says I'm an awful player. I'm so stupid." He sighs and says, "Maybe I should just quit hockey and . . ."

He wipes his face with a tissue, straightens up, and with a gentle "please help me" look says, "But I love being with my friends and I love playing hockey. Can you help me make my dad happy with me?"

Jeremy's thinking, *I really want to please Dad, I really want to be a good hockey player, I really want to be good, but I can't. I'm stupid.* This type of thinking is toxic to a child's emotional health. And it doesn't need to happen.

Let's listen as Dad weighs in now. His story paints quite a different picture.

"This is Jeremy's sixth year in hockey. By age fourteen, he should be coming into his own. I go to every game, I spend a lot of money on out-of-town trips, gear, and so on—and I really work hard to help him. He just doesn't put effort into what I tell him to do—on anything, but especially hockey. And everyone says he's got the makings of a pro. I'm just about done. I'm so frustrated and I don't know what else to do."

Dad's message: *I'm working so hard to help Jeremy, but he's not improving, and I'm feeling like a failure.* And he's been feeling this for about two years. He has no energy left.

Do Dad and Jeremy seem like two ships passing in the night? Thanks to Mr. Longfellow for this great word picture. He probably knew all about this sort of thing, having raised six kids and grown up in a family of eight kids. He described brilliantly what often happens in every parent's 25/8 job:

> *We pass and speak to one another,*
>
> *only a look and a voice,*
>
> *then darkness again and a silence.*

Both Dad and Jeremy are in the dark about each other's concerns.

Here's the problem: Dad's ship is focused on Jeremy's *outside* stuff—his performance. Jeremy's ship is focused on two *inside* things: (1) trying to please Dad and (2) wanting to feel he's an overall okay, likeable boy. Jeremy believes *I can't be okay if Dad thinks I'm not.*

Until communication improves, Dad's and Jeremy's points will go unrecognized and unresolved. They'll miss each other like those two passing ships. Dad will only get more frustrated, and Jeremy's belief that he's no good will only get worse.

I don't know about you, but I find it's really hard to focus on another person's inside feelings and thoughts when all I can see is how right I am. I can think of several situations that occurred while my four children were growing up in which I missed their points completely. Later I got to experience the uncomfortable, sometimes unpleasant, consequences of insisting on my way. Perhaps you can think of similar circumstances in your own life. Instead of beating ourselves up, however, let's take a deep breath and accept that it's just human nature to push our own points too much.

Fortunately, we don't have to be held hostage by our human nature. Let's get busy applying ways to help our children feel okay about themselves even when they're messing up. We'll start with the main point of this chapter: *Your child's deep-down biggest motivator is to be good.* I know, the outside behavior—arguing, yelling, refusing to do chores, and so on—sure doesn't send that message. But the rest of this chapter will help you see and tap into this powerful "I want to be good" motivator. As you begin to apply the principles you'll read in the next several pages, many of your parenting "failures" will fade away and you and your child will actually begin enjoying each other's company and have a lot more fun together.

Below are the three points we'll cover in detail that will help shed light on the inside part of your child:

1. Children want to be good for their parents; it's a primary life motivator.
2. Parents determine what good means by their words, facial expressions, tone of voice, and their attention to a child's developmental stage.
3. Three top tips for making *I'm a good kid* stick: Find the good; parent for success; and spend time, not money.

Children Want to Be Good, Especially for Their Parents

When parents hear for the first time that their children really want to be good even when they are misbehaving, they give me that "you must not have kids" look. Then they ask, "How can you tell me my preschooler wants to be *good*? I get at least one call every week from his teacher about how he's throwing things, biting kids, or screaming—and nothing I do stops it."

Or how about this one: "I've been working for a year now trying to get my middleschooler to do all her homework, but every week she has at least two missing assignments. And then she has the gall to think I'll believe her lies about losing her papers."

I'm sure you see similar behaviors from time to time in your family; your child knows what good behavior is, but she doesn't put it into practice and nothing you do makes a difference. You think, *She can't want to be good or she'd change, right? She's just stubborn or probably lazy. Worse yet, she may never learn to be responsible. This wanting-to-be-good stuff sounds like psychobabble.*

I can understand your skepticism. As a parent, I've been there too. But here's what you may not see: Your child's unbending behavior is just the tip of the iceberg. And at the bottom of the iceberg you'll find *I want to be good.* Unfortunately, we don't often get to the bottom because we don't typically accept and deal with what's in between—the submerged thoughts and feelings, our child's inside stuff.

So how do we accept and deal with that middle chunk of the ice? The answer's in the Golden Rule: "Treat others the same way you want them to treat you." We all would love to be treated as though we're basically okay. Even when we've made a mistake. Accepting your child's inside feelings and thoughts is the key, and when you do, all kinds of positive changes happen.

Remember Jeremy's hockey situation? Dad's been chipping away at the tip of the problem and completely missing Jeremy's inside stuff.

To get a better grasp of the center of the iceberg, let's all pile into our custom-made psych-marine and take a quick look at what's below Jeremy's hockey problem. Before we give the "dive" order, let's stay on deck and take a look at that icy tip—Jeremy's "awful" hockey skills. Dad's chipping efforts haven't made a bit of difference, and the boy is frustrated. *Exasperated,* the Scriptures call it. The situation seems hopeless, at least at the surface.

Now, everyone below. Settle in as we take a below-the-surface tour and get ready to hear Jeremy's feelings and thoughts through our state-of-the-art surround-sound system. As we listen in, keep in mind that our feelings and thoughts

- play a huge role in determining how we act.
- represent the epicenter, the heart, of who we are. They're a big energy source for what we do; they tell us what our most im-

portant beliefs are, our essential how-to-live-right guidelines. And they're the most accurate in-depth signal of who we are on a minute-to-minute basis. No wonder kids like adults to pay attention to their feelings!

- must be identified and supported before discipline occurs. A space-shuttle commander wouldn't even think of lifting off without completing his preflight checklist of internal systems. (That's the main reason our discipline "blastoff" efforts fail; we don't adequately deal with the inside systems of feelings and thoughts.)

Okay, the audio's turned up; let's listen to Jeremy's feeling and thinking. He's actually in his room now, replaying the shouting match that occurred in the car.

Dad says, "Your defense skills are awful. That player you let get around you? Why on earth did . . .?"

Jeremy's heart beats faster, his fists clench, and he thinks, *I'd like to hit Dad. No, I can't. I can't yell and I can't cry. Gotta bite my lip—hard. I'm awful. I'll never do it right for Dad.*

Dad yells through Jeremy's thoughts, "What's wrong with you? Are you hearing me? Answer me and don't cry!" This is not the way Jeremy needs to be treated. Dad has violated the Golden Rule.

Jeremy can't remember any more, but between his angry reflections he thinks, *I've got to improve. I've got to find a way to make Dad like me. What am I going to do? I can't stop the tears. I can't do anything right.*

Let's turn the audio off even though Jeremy is generating a lot more thoughts. (Experts estimate that most people have about forty thoughts every minute.) We've got Jeremy's bottom-line message: *I want to be good for Dad, I'm panicking because I can't be good, and I'm just a no-good person.*

And here's the Psych 101 explanation for what's happening with every kid in this type of situation: Children develop beliefs about themselves primarily through their parents' responses to them. When parents focus primarily on negatives, children will develop negative beliefs about themselves. And the fundamental need to be good—to please parents and feel like an okay person—is squelched.

Hey, Kids!

Kids, did you know your feelings were that important? It really does hurt a lot when Mom and Dad yell at you, doesn't it? I know, parents always say, "I'm not yelling." Anyway, you feel horrible. And sometimes it happens a lot and you really feel bad a lot, but you just want to feel you're an okay kid. Does that sound confusing? I know it can, because I talk to kids every day about this stuff, and I also remember feeling this way as a kid (even though I was a kid a long time ago).

Let's make this simple: Mom and Dad really do need to listen carefully to your feelings and believe them. (They'll do a lot more of this in the future because they're reading this book.) When they take your feelings seriously, you'll feel understood and you'll feel a lot more okay about yourself. Really, it'll happen.

I hope this is making sense. When we stop and reflect, I think all of us know feelings and thoughts really are powerful. But isn't it interesting that so little public attention is paid to this truth? When's the last time you saw a CNN headline: BREAKING NEWS—*Warning to parents: not validating feelings increases risks for raising an unhealthy kid*. Sound silly, doesn't it? Gives you kind of a sinking feeling to realize how our society ignores what's really important.

You, however, are paying attention to what's important: your child. So, how do you pull off the complicated task of correcting your child while simultaneously helping your child feel *I'm okay*? Read on.

How to Make Your Child Feel Good When She's Bad

Seeing that bold subtitle that ends with "she's bad" (substitute "he's" if you have a son) kind of stabs you in the gut, doesn't it? Why does it sound so awful? For me, it's because feeling bad is so ugly—for both children and adults. We don't like it, and it's the last thing we want our kids to feel. And kids feel *I'm bad* way more than you would ever imagine!

I know, I've been on submarine duty for more than forty years. I hear it every day and it hurts every time.

But here's the truth from the mouths of the many children I've counseled: When kids are wrong and corrected too much, they all feel, in one way or another, *I'm bad*. They don't think, *I know I have ADHD, and it's hard to behave, and my mom and dad are just doing what's best for me*. No, children are black and white thinkers. When children don't please their parents enough, they develop a deep-seated belief of *I'm bad*. And here's the way they'll express it: "You don't understand me"; "You always yell at me"; or "Sis never gets yelled at." Or worse, "I don't care anymore." "I don't care" comments mean a child has given up on wanting to be good. These are the kids who often become bullies or may develop clinical depression because they feel hopeless.

We all hear these comments from our children from time to time. When you do, don't panic, but do be just a tad nervous. Even if your child says these things often, the material in this book will fix the problem for most families. (Remember, seek counseling if you don't make enough progress.) So that I don't put too much sugar on these points, let me make this recommendation: When your child makes these "I'm bad" comments, shift your focus from the misbehavior to the inside feelings and thoughts. It's in this deep-down-inside world of feelings that you'll be able to establish your child's belief of *I'm okay*.

Here's the main point of this section: Your child's *I'm okay* feeling is determined by *you*. Sounds overwhelming, I know. But it really doesn't need to be so daunting when you use these three strategies in your effort to establish *I'm a good person* deep within your child:

1. Fit your expectations to your child's developmental stage and personality.
2. Remember that your facial expression and tone of voice speak louder than your words.
3. Focus on and validate your child's feelings first, then deal with the behavior. When you do, you're communicating to your child's heart. You're saying, "You're okay deep inside; now let's learn appropriate behavior."

Realistic Expectations

The result of setting realistic expectations? Success, a lot of it. Is there a better motivator? In kid's lingo: *I'm good because I'm pleasing Mom and Dad a lot.* The Golden Rule's doing its miracle.

Four-year-old Graham is trying everything out for the first time: how words work, what happens when he pulls Kitty's tail, and what a bummer it is to pick up toys—all typical things for a child his age. This behavior can get frustrating for Mom and Dad, and before they know it, they have made yelling a habit. Graham thinks, *When Dad yells at me it really upsets me. Maybe he doesn't like me.* (Again, kids think black or white—they think they're either good or bad, with no in between.) The key here is this: *Make at least 75 percent of your daily interactions positive.* (Don't feel bad if you have some 35 percent days; they happen to all of us. Kids are not fragile if they feel *good enough* most of the time.)

Dad's read all about what a big deal self-doubt is at this age, and he really tries to be more positive than negative. Dad also knows Graham's personality: he's really emotional and very active. (How to fit your parenting approach to your child's unique personality is the subject of the next chapter.) It is critical that Dad not be *too* critical.

What about expectations for your six-to-twelve-year-old? Becky's first day at school is her chance to try out her independence. It's the first time she gets to test some new skills and learn how good she is at making friends in a large group. The big thing she's learning: *It's really important to try new things and not feel inferior when I fail. (Am I competent or inferior?* That's what this age range is all about, according to Erik Erikson (best known for his theory of the stages of human development). Expectations set by parents need to foster many successful independent experiences.

What about the middle school years? Connor's had a lot of success trying new things, but friendships have been a problem. He's found out the reason from the school counselor. (Don't hesitate to use a counselor at your child's school as a resource when trouble pops up.) Connor's shy personality causes him to not reach out to other kids, and he's alone way too much—not a good feeling much of the time. (Golden Rule point: Being liked by peers is important for kids developmentally; they need to experience being treated this way.) *Nobody likes me* changed when Mom and Dad got Connor into wrestling. There he established several lasting friendships and, you guessed it, *I'm okay* became a deep-seated feeling.

Hey, Kids!

Kids, do you think there's stuff about you that's way too different or weird, like your freckles or nobody wanting to play with you? Ask your parents about these worries. (Parents, you might want to read chapter 4, about your child's unique personality, before answering this question.)

Did you know everyone's different? And sometimes there will be things about you that people don't like. But those things can be fixed! Yeah, that's right. I know what I'm talking about. For example, I've had ADHD my whole life. I was one of those kids who's all over the place, the kid nobody really wants to be around. When I was younger, most adults didn't like me because I was always talking and interrupting them. I felt really dumb and bad. But when I found out why I did those things, I was able to improve a lot with adults helping me. You can do the same. Ask your parents to help you.

Parents, I'm sure you're getting the drift. When you're yelling too much and you're not making progress with your child (and I can assure you, yelling is *never* conducive to progress), turn everything off and take a walk around the situation. Do your expectations fit your child's personality and developmental stage? Make some parenting adjustments and find several positive things about your child (character qualities, accomplishments, things he or she has done right) that you can focus on. Search harder¬¬--they're there! Ask God to help you find and acknowledge all the good, positive things you've tended to overlook. Then try again, complimenting your child on the positives. Your goal is to help your child feel successful 75 percent of the time. With that foundation in place, he or she will feel better understood and more willing to deal with the corrective teaching of the moment.

Let's take a quick look at the adolescent years. First, make sure you've figured out your teen's personality traits and how to fit into them in the best way possible. (Chapter 4 gives you all the tips you'll need on this one.) Second, realize that the teen mindset can be summed up like this: *Now I can do everything by myself; don't get in my way; I know everything.*

When working with teens, you can count on three things. First, expect self-centeredness. That's your teen's way of really knowing *who I am.* Second, rebellion is the norm. Your teen is thinking, *I need to be different and see how the test drive goes.* And third, expect a teen to think two opposite ways at the same time (ambivalence) even if he doesn't express both thoughts. He may say, "I think marijuana should be legalized," as if that's his only opinion. However, deep inside, usually not even consciously, he's thinking, *I know marijuana's not good for the brain.*

Don't fight these three developmental behaviors. Instead, work with them. For self-centeredness, acknowledge Liz's not wanting to be at Friday family dinners but require her presence anyway. For rebellion, allow Stephen to give his opposite view that Democrats are better than Republicans (or vice versa, depending on your political persuasion, because you can expect him to favor the party you don't support). Remember that you're not agreeing; you're listening, treating your teen the way you want to be treated. And by the way, research shows that the best place to fully explore different ideas is with the family.

Last, for ambivalence, count on Ronda having an opposite opinion—down deep inside—from the one she's giving voice to: "I think we should sell our house and car and move to Kenya to protect endangered animals there." Golden Rule point: People like to feel they're being listened to and understood. Most of the time decisions and disagreement can wait until these two really important needs are adequately met.

Maybe you're starting to feel as though you need an advanced academic degree to pull this off. I agree that it can feel a little complicated. But here are a couple ways to make Golden-Rule parenting doable. First, think about putting one knee in front of the other. You don't need to even take baby steps—just crawl! Second, stick with it, and you'll soon get the hang of it. I often tell parents, "If you end up doing these things 60 percent of the time, you qualify for the Great Parent award."

That's it for realistic expectations, the linchpin of it all. Just remember, when you're teaching good behavior, take your child's personality and developmental needs into account. As you fit your parenting approach to your child's personality, your child will think something like this: *When you treat me with understanding, I can learn a lot better about being good, and it feels good to please you.* Thanks, Golden Rule.

Now let's take a look at how our face and voice impact "I'm okay."

Facial Expression and Voice Tone

None of us likes to hear a negative tone, especially when we've messed up. Any expression of *excessive* anger signals "I'm bad" to a child. Mild anger, firm voice and words—that's part of setting firm limits. But yell too much, too often, and you won't be tapping into your child's deep inner desire to be good.

Scientists say angry facial expressions are as powerful as using negative, judgmental words such as *stupid* or *lazy*. The opposite is true of happy facial expressions, like smiling. A smile stimulates the pleasure part of the brain. No, you don't have to grit your teeth and grin when you'd rather be scowling. But there is an out: Don't attempt discipline when you're upset. And work on mixing in some pleasant facial expressions when you're disciplining. Tell your arguing child the experiences you had arguing as a child, and chuckle a bit as you relate the story.

Now let's take a quick look at the importance of dealing with feelings first before we discipline. I know we've covered a lot already about feelings, but the topic needs continued attention because it's so important for establishing your child's belief of *I'm good.*

Feelings Before Discipline

Dealing with feelings is the first key to grab when you're ready to start disciplining. When your child's messing up, remember that feelings are at the bottom of the behavior and those feelings need to be acknowledged and validated. This isn't a typical parenting approach (focusing only on behavior change), but then you're not the typical parent!

Check out the two approaches. The *behavior-only approach*: "Anthony, you keep fighting your 8:30 bedtime. Get to bed now or you lose your TV time tomorrow." (Talking, no listening.) The *feelings approach* looks like this: "Anthony, tell me what you feel about your 8:30 bedtime." After you hear all his points you say, "Let's move it to 8:45, but you need to get up with one wakeup call in the morning without arguing. If you do that, I'll make the 8:45 bedtime permanent." (A lot of listening, a little talking.) Of course, you'll need to stand your ground most of the time, but occasionally changing your mind really makes kids feel good. They think, *Who I am, different from Mom and Dad, is sometimes okay.*

So here's the point: When you make feelings okay first and then correct behavior, you've solved the age-old problem of helping your child feel good even when he's being bad. We all want to be treated like we're basically okay even when we make a mistake. It's the Golden Rule to the rescue: *When you treat me like I'm not totally messed up, I feel like working harder to be good.*

Hey, Kids!

Kids, I know doing the right thing usually is really boring. As your mom and dad are trying to help you feel that you're not some weirdo when you mess up, guess what you need to do a lot more often? Put a lot of effort into doing what Mom and Dad ask you to do—right away. Especially with the boring stuff, like picking up after yourself. Hard to believe this is important, but it is. Remember, do important boring stuff, and everything goes a lot better. Hang in there; you'll be on your own in ten years or so.

Parents, it seems like you have a lot to do right, doesn't it? Remember, do it right 60 percent of the time, and that's good enough. So turn the heat to medium on your pressure cooker with these two tips: First, pick one thing to work on—maybe less yelling, for example; second, give yourself a three-week break-in time—the "one knee in front of the other" approach.

Now we're ready to conclude this chapter with three short and sweet tips—just in case you run out of things to do.

Three Top "I Like Myself" Tips

To help your child develop healthier self-esteem, you can't go wrong if prioritize the following three areas of your relationship:

1. *Find the good.* Make a good-qualities list about your child: friendly, funny, caring, and so forth. Don't let a day go by without at least one positive comment that reflects some characteristic from the list, such as "Your brother sure liked you helping him put on his shoes." Follow the "4 to 1" rule: four positive comments to one negative. That's a big turn-around from what's typical: five negatives to one positive.

2. *Parent for success.* At the *beginning* of a problem, make sure the solution has a 98 percent chance of being successful. After all, who doesn't like success? For example, your child's not good at math, and those twenty-problem assignments are dreadful. Reduce the work by half after you've got the teacher's thumbs up. Get a week of your child feeling *I'm okay* with the reduced workload, and then start getting your child as close as possible to doing the full assignment. (Chapter 5 is all about the power of success.)

3. *Spend time, not money.* Do you know that a child's—even a teen's—priority is family time? In kids' lingo, "I wish my dad didn't work so much"; or "I really like our Friday family dinner where everyone gets to say what was fun during the week."

   Why is time spent with kids such a big deal? Whether they admit to it or not, kids want to please and be liked by their parents. Time together sends this message: "My mom thinks I'm really important and likes to spend time with me." Start with these guidelines: fifteen minutes of undivided attention two school nights a week doing something your child likes to do. Then, once a month, spend one half-day away from the house doing what's fun for your child (don't drop by Home Depot). Your time translates into *I'm likable.*

That's it for this chapter, the first week of test driving the Golden Rule way of parenting. We've covered some really important Golden Rule material in the first three chapters: Chapter 1 explored how children want to be understood; chapter 2 helped you learn to begin where your children are; and in chapter 3 we've gone below the surface to realize that children really want to be good, and they want their parents to treat them this way.

Now it's time for week two, the put-on-your-work-clothes-and-gloves part. You'll get a great toolbox full of tried and tested tools, forged through more than forty years of counseling, that will help you help your child become the best person possible. We'll start out with where your child is at the most basic level.

Life goes a lot more smoothly when you're in tune with your child's unique personality traits.

WEEK 2

"... And Help Me Become a Better Person"

How Your Child Wants to Be Treated (Part II)

CHAPTER 4: "Please Discipline Me, but According to
My Personality"

CHAPTER 5: "Please Enhance My Chances of Success"

CHAPTER 6: "I Need for Us to Agree to Disagree Agreeably"

CHAPTER 4

"Please Discipline Me, but According to My Personality"

TREAT CHILDREN THE WAY *I would like to be treated.*

Isn't it interesting how one single short sentence can pack such a treasure trove of parenting gems? And you don't even need the Internet to know how to treat your child; just do a quick self-Google of "how I want to be treated." The speed's really fast, the information is as detailed as you want it to be, and it's free!

Here's a fast recap of the search results we've found so far: Everyone wants to be treated with understanding and acceptance, especially when being corrected. And the key to pulling this off during discipline is to listen to, understand, and validate your child's feelings *before* correcting the problem. The big bonus? Your child feels understood, and your child's need to be good is met a lot faster. Your child feels *I'm really okay even when I'm in trouble.*

Is it possible to make discipline even less bumpy? Yes, with another Golden Rule parenting gem we'll cover in this chapter: *Attune your parenting approach to your child's unique personality traits.*

Let's do another quick self-Google search of your own childhood experiences: "Mom and Dad's attunement to my personality traits." How did your mom's frustration feel when you always pushed for your way of doing things (ranking high on the trait of persistence)? Or maybe you got really upset when routines changed, especially when no one told you (ranking low on the trait of adaptability). And your dad always frowned at you and griped, "Why do you always make such a big deal about stopping what you're doing when we need to go someplace?" How about your cautiousness at trying new things or warming up to people (ranking high on the trait of withdrawal)? You often heard your mom complaining, "I don't get why you avoid everything." There is no attunement from the parents in any of these examples, but there was certainly a lot of inside negative thinking on your part: *There must be something wrong with me.*

Just as a well-tuned orchestra delivers beautiful music, a parent's attunement with a child's personality produces a harmonious relationship and gives your child a solid sense of being acceptable. Your child feels, *When you accept me the way I am down deep inside, I can learn to really like myself, warts and all.*

Before tackling this attunement business, let's first set the stage for this week's subject: fulfilling your child's true inner desire to become a better person. This is the part of the book that deals with discipline, the Golden Rule way. We'll cover three often-ignored but crucial facets of loving, effective discipline: (1) attune to your child's personality, (2) tap into the power of success, and (3) disagree agreeably. When we boil it down, discipline involves changing the way we think and behave. It's a daily struggle for everyone to be a better person and a task that's in front of us 25/8 with our children. Decreasing the "heavy lifting" involved will be a welcome relief—and what I hope you'll experience after acquiring the skills outlined in this section of the book.

Now we're ready for our journey into the world of parent-child attunement. Let's pile into our electric-powered, double-decker observation bus and take a tour of two typical family situations where we'll see personality traits in full bloom. The families are wired for audio (both their outside conversations and their inside feelings), and there are hidden cameras in each room. (Yes, we have their permission to watch everything.) Oh, put on your blood-pressure cuffs. You might be surprised at your stress level as you watch the ways these families interact.

We've got about three minutes before we arrive at our first home, so take a quick look at the personality-trait cheat sheet you almost sat on when you boarded. Everyone is born with nine traits, and everyone has his or her own inborn way of expressing them. Let's look at INTENSITY OF REACTION, for example. Laura cries at the drop of a hat even though she's twelve years old. Her dad's the complete opposite of his daughter; he never cries and always stays cool as a cucumber. Typically, these differing personalities clash. Dad regularly gets upset with Becky: "I don't understand why you're such a crybaby." Laura feels bad and Dad's frustrated. After Dad learns to become attuned to Laura's intensity, his frustration will decrease a lot. The rest of the chapter is full of attunement "how-tos" for you to test drive with your child.

Keep the following trait list handy while we listen in to these two families and try to identify which traits apply:

The Nine Personality Traits

1. ACTIVITY LEVEL
2. REGULARITY
3. ADAPTABILITY
4. APPROACH/WITHDRAWAL
5. PHYSICAL SENSITIVITY
6. INTENSITY OF REACTION
7. DISTRACTIBILITY
8. POSITIVE OR NEGATIVE MOOD
9. PERSISTENCE

This list was developed years ago by two researchers, Alexander Thomas and Stella Chess. What a great contribution to helping us understand children and everyone else: *Your child was born with his or her particular intensity levels for each trait.* If your daughter is highly distractible, for example, she was born that way. You didn't have anything to do with developing that quality in her. Her distractibility level is not your fault. Most parents are relieved to learn they are not totally responsible for how their child turns out.

<u>The Sherman Family</u>

Okay, we're pulling up to our parking place a block from our first family's home. We're just in time to catch the Shermans' early morning drama.

Dad shuts off his annoying alarm, but down the hall another alarm's still blaring. Dad turns to Mom and says, "It's your turn to battle Sasha's morning madness."

Mom groans. "Yeah, I know." She throws off the blankets, grabs her robe, and shuffles down to her daughter's room, thinking, *We're a month into her sixth grade year, and like everything else, getting up's a battle. She yells no matter what. Sometimes she's fine—eventually—but most of the time we get surprise grenades lobbed at us.*

This time I'll not yell back. As Mom shuts off the alarm, she looks at Sasha. *If she could only maintain that slumberland peacefulness.* Mom gently rubs Sasha's arm and whispers, "Sasha . . ."

Sasha shoves Mom's hand away and mumbles, "No, I'm not getting up. Leave me alone."

"I'm setting the—"

Sasha covers her head and screams, "I don't care about the stupid timer!"

Mom's heart beats faster and she sets the timer, saying nothing as she lowers her head, hunches her shoulders, and leaves the room.

The timer goes off, and round two begins. Mom walks into Sasha's room and Sasha says, "You can't make me get up."

At least she's awake. Mom stands still, barely breathing, and says nothing—something new she's trying.

After several "you can't make me" comments, Sasha sits up in bed, points stiff-armed toward the door, and yells, "Go! Leave me alone."

Success! Mom knows once Sasha is vertical, getting dressed will eventually happen. Mom leaves without yelling, thinking, *Whew! I did it.* She starts breakfast and mentally prepares for round three.

Sasha rolls up into a ball underneath her comfy covers. *Mom's always yelling at me. She never yells at Darin. He always does everything right, never talks back. I can't stop yelling. What's wrong with me? Got to get up before Dad comes in.* She throws the covers off, gets up, kicks the bedpost, and quickly puts on her clothes. But not quickly enough. Sure thing, Dad's at the door yelling, "We'll be late to school if we don't eat now." Sasha yells back, "Leave me alone!"

A few minutes later, Sasha goes to the table, her eyes avoiding everything but the carpet as she walks. Once seated, she scowls at her eggs as she eats.

Dad tries to make conversation; sometimes it helps, other times things get worse. "Are things going any better with Amie?"

"No. Nobody likes me." Tears well up, Sasha's voice elevates, and she strikes the table with her fist. "Nobody plays with me and nobody wants to sit with me at lunch." She thinks, *I hate school. It's so lonely. Nobody wants me and Mom and Dad are always against me.*

Mom and Dad glance at each other, hearts aching, both thinking the same thing: *Hardly anything is positive in her life. Will she ever stop being so sensitive and negative?*

That's the morning at the Sherman house. So, how's your blood pressure? Have you identified the problem personality traits? Maybe you don't have a child with all those problems, but most of us have been in this type of position. Whatever our child is going through, we hurt for him, and nothing we do seems to change anything. We feel so helpless. Worse, we begin to feel that the child's negative behavior is purposeful. Let me assure you, however, that most of the time a big portion of your child's behavior is related to inborn temperament-trait problems, and dealing with those problems requires a different discipline approach—one that is attuned to the specific trait problem.

Let's fast forward to later in the day.

Dad has decided to try something different when he picks up Sasha from school. He's inviting her to her favorite ice cream shop. Sasha walks slowly to the car, alone again. She gets in, crosses her arms tightly, frowns with all her strength, and glares straight out the window.

Dad dispenses with the "how's your day" routine, which would only get her started on how bad her day was. "How about Jerry and Bob's ice cream? They've got Mint Delight, your favorite."

Sasha looks up, her expression starts to change, and finally she breaks into a grin. "Yeah, Dad, let's go."

Dad's heart expands. *Bingo! Did something right. If I could only make it happen more often.* At the ice cream place, Dad tries something new—talking about what Sash likes best about school, her drawing class. Sasha opens up, and the two of them have a really pleasant conversation.

Now skip to Saturday morning. Sasha's favorite activity is to watch cartoons. This morning, though, TV time has to be cut short because the family is going out to brunch. Mom forgot to tell Sasha, who is thirty-five minutes into her favorite show.

Mom knows that's trouble, but she has no choice but to break the news: "Sasha we need to get dressed. We're—"

"No. This is my favorite program." After a ten-minute skirmish, Sasha stomps to her room and eventually gets dressed.

Sasha is miserable to be with on the way to the restaurant, and she does no better throughout the meal: sour face, no eye contact, clipped answers, and embarrassed parents. For as long as Mom and Dad can remember, whenever they've had to ask Sasha to suddenly switch activities, this has been her typical response.

What have you learned from our observations of the Shermans? (Maybe you've learned you need blood pressure medication!) Certainly, we know Sasha's parents need to attune their parenting to Sasha's problems. How? First they need to take a look at the personality trait list and see which traits are too intense.

1. *ACTIVITY LEVEL?* No big deal.

2. *REGULARITY* (predictability of physical things like eating, restroom habits, or sleep-wake cycle)? There's definitely a problem with wake-up times.

3. *ADAPTABILITY* (ease of changing from one thing to another)? Big problem with this trait.

4. *APPROACH/AVOIDANCE* (how easily a person engages with people or activities)? Sasha definitely avoids solving problems; she has relationship issues at school and at home.

5. *PHYSICAL SENSITIVITY* (degree of sensitivity to taste, sight, hearing, smell, touch)? No information to evaluate.

6. *INTENSITY OF REACTION* (amount of emotional intensity and sensitivity)? This trait is the biggest problem of all.

7. *DISTRACTIBILITY* (maintaining attention)? Not enough information.

8. *MOOD*—POSITIVE OR NEGATIVE (a person's overall outlook on life, positive or negative)? Negative attitude is a huge problem.

9. *PERSISTENCE* (degree of stick-to-itiveness)? Sasha's more on the high side; she pushes for her way but usually ends up doing what she was supposed to do.

So what's the bottom line? Sasha and her parents are struggling mightily with five personality trait problems: REGULARITY, ADAPTABILITY, APPROACH/AVOIDANCE, INTENSITY OF REACTION, and MOOD. Children who struggle with these five traits are considered "difficult" children and comprise about 10 percent of the population. (HIGH ACTIVITY LEVEL is another trait that's typically included in the difficult-child trait list.) Of course, your child doesn't need to demonstrate all five problem traits for life to be difficult. Just dealing with one trait can be a full-time job. Maybe your child is a drama queen (INTENSITY OF REACTION), or your child's attitude is mostly negative (MOOD). Those are tough traits to handle day after day.

If you have a difficult child, there is hope! You'll see firsthand in the rest of this chapter how the intensity of these traits can be noticeably reduced when you fit your parenting approach into your child's difficult traits.

Often, parents think attunement means permissive parenting— letting your child do whatever he or she feels like doing. No, setting firm limits is critical. But here's the attunement key: *Discipline needs to be done with more positive than negative interactions.* You can do this by modifying your expectations to provide a better fit with your child's problem personality traits.

When a persistent problem grinds on, negative parental interactions are typically at least 75 percent of the total daily parent-child exchanges. It's just the way we're made: A child's negative behavior automatically results in negative parental responses. When we're stuck and continually failing, it seems impossible to be constructive and uplifting by finding positive ways to discipline or focusing on positive qualities. Parenting becomes miserable.

Hey, Kids!

Kids, how do you like being called a "difficult child?" It's awful! Most of you know you're not pleasing your parents, and you find yourself yelling or being difficult way too much of the time. It's really hard to stop. And here's what kids tell me upsets them most: "Everyone says you ought to be able to stop, and when you don't, teachers and parents get really mad and disappointed in you. And what's really a bummer is that this stuff seems to never stop."

Here's what I want you to know: *Down deep inside, you're really good enough and really worth liking.* I can just hear you saying, "Yeah, right. I never hear that from anybody, especially my mom and dad. And even if I am good enough, nobody acts like I am."

Here's something else: The wrong stuff you say and do is really just a small part of you, even though your negative behavior is all people seem to notice. There really are a lot of good things about you. By reading this book, your mom and dad are learning how to help you reduce the wrong things in a positive way and focus more on what's good about you. I know you'll really enjoy being treated this way.

Parents, does applying this negative-to-positive Golden Rule approach to discipline sound too tough to do with a difficult child? It does to most parents, until they learn three important parenting skills that help turbo-charge their attunement efforts. Here they are, applied to the Sherman family.

Skill 1: Love and Affection

According to Robert Epstein's 2010 study, expressing love and affection is the number-one-ranked parenting skill. We've learned a lot about this skill already. Understanding your child is one of the most loving things you can do for your child. And plenty of positive one-to-one time sprinkled with physical affection really drives home "I love you." It's the fastest route for children to believe *I'm okay* and to feel down-deep security.

But how do Sasha's parents show understanding with such negative behavior? They're already making headway: Dad initiated the father-daughter ice cream date, and Mom's showing understanding when she holds back negative comments regarding Sasha's wake-up difficulty. (Eventually Sasha will need to learn how to translate her negative behavior and comments into positive feeling words, but she's not ready for this step just yet.) And there's a lot more Mom and Dad can do to become better attuned to Sasha that will result in better behavior, such as preparing her ahead of time for stopping her Saturday morning cartoons so the family can be on time for an outing.

Often parents think, *Most of this behavior is just purposeful, mean choices.* I don't blame them for feeling this way. The behavior does look totally purposeful, and at times it is on purpose. But most of the time the misbehavior is a personality-trait problem and requires discipline that addresses the specific trait problem.

You might be thinking you need a PhD to become an "attuned parent." Don't apply for the degree just yet. With practice you'll get more comfortable with this skill. There'll be many more "how-to" attunement illustrations for you to apply to your child throughout the following chapters.

Skill 2: Stress Management

Stress management is Epstein's number-two-ranked parenting skill. Too much stress is unhealthy. Physically, in times of excessive stress, our bodies release too much cortisol (stress hormone), which is detrimental to the immune and endocrine systems. Excessive anger and disappointment directed toward children increases the risk of making them feel bad too often. Pay close attention to these two things: (1) keep *your* stress level down in your daily life—your child is watching and taking it all in—and (2) teach your child to keep stress low. Here are a few stress-management tips for Sasha's dad to follow:

- Approach each day––and especially each provocative situation with your child––with proactive prayer, asking God to keep you calm and in control of your emotions no matter what kind of misbehavior or attitude your child exhibits. The Bible assures followers that the fruit of the Holy Spirit in one's life includes love, peace, patience, gentleness, and self-control (see Galatians 5:22–23 for the full list of qualities). Through prayer, trust God to give you the grace and wisdom you need to handle the situation.

- Agree to leave the situation when frustration is too high (yelling, arguing) and deal with the problem later without excessive anger. Mom's already doing this successfully.

- Teach and model relaxation exercises: diaphragm breathing, progressive muscle relaxation, or meditation. Sasha needs to be taught these skills—when she's calm.

- Balance play and work. Always mix in plenty of laughter and humor throughout your daily interactions. With this healthy effort, life really can be fun most of the time. Sasha's dad did this with the ice cream date. Humor needs to be used a lot more.

Sasha's temperament traits spell stress for both her and her parents. But attunement to these traits *will* reduce the stress. Here's a quick reminder about two of the most important attunement pointers. First, remember that Sasha's not purposefully being mean all the time; it's mostly her personality. Second, tune in to her ADAPTABILITY and INTENSITY OF REACTION traits by changing expectations: Give early warnings for changed routine, help Sasha transform mean yelling into words like "I'm really mad." (Feelings words help decrease excessive frustration.)

And here's a basic *must* when frustration starts to escalate: *Leave the situation.* It's really hard to do at first (who doesn't want to get in the last word?). But as you practice, your frustration will decrease significantly. Here's your short and sweet stress-management motto: *We solve problems when we're calm, not upset.*

Skill 3: Behavior Management

Behavior management is Epstein's number-nine-ranked parenting skill. The majority of parents would rank consequences, time-outs, and all the other behavior-management skills as number one because they're an essential part of parenting. Teaching our children to manage their behavior has to begin very early in their lives. Why? Because we're born to live life "my way." It takes eighteen years of acquiring behavior-management skills to learn the right balance between "my way" and "your way." No wonder parenting feels so overwhelming at times.

Sasha needs a lot of help managing her behavior. Typical consequences such as timeouts, deprivation, and rewards are the way to go, but in order to work effectively they must be attuned to Sasha's temperament traits. For starters, I'd recommend a two-week reward program for getting out of bed without hostile words. Instead of saying, "Get out of my room," Sasha can learn to say, in a more civil voice, "I'm mad at you." You may be thinking, *Why reward her for what she should be doing anyway?* Harnessing the INTENSITY OF REACTION trait, especially angry outbursts, requires high levels of motivation, particularly during the early learning stages. Rewards fit the bill. (More on rewards in the next chapter, where we'll cover the power of success.)

Here are three quick consequence tips for Sasha's parents to use, just in case they run out of things to work on: (1) Pick only one battle a week (four victories a month is nothing to sneeze at); (2) follow through, always; and (3) fit expectations into Sasha's normal need for independence during her tween years—give her choices to make her feel powerful in a healthy way.

That's it for our visit to the Sherman home. What do you think of this attunement approach for your child? Have you figured out yet what's at the bottom of being attuned to your child? It's simply *acceptance—accepting your child for who he or she is right now.* Don't we all want to be accepted for who we really are?

Here's what I hear over and over from children whose parents use this approach: "My parents have helped me understand why I'm different from other kids. Now I accept who I am, and I really want to improve myself." Feeling different without understanding is a self-esteem buster. Feeling different with understanding raises self-worth and self-confidence.

The Thomas Family

Let's move on to our second home visit. We're going to observe the Thomas family with their only child, five-year-old Nat. Nat's mom and dad don't know it, but his traits qualify him as an "easy child" (40 percent of all children fit this category). His activity level is moderate, his regularity is the way it's supposed to be, he easily adapts to changes most of the time, he typically approaches new things with enthusiasm, and his mood is almost always positive.

But Nat's parents do have some challenges. They've just finished a parenting attunement class. Let's take a quick look-see at what they've learned.

Every Saturday morning seems to bring the same situation: The house is a mess and needs to be cleaned (Mom's frequently out of town on business), Friday night dishes need to be done, groceries need to be purchased, and more. It's already 10 a.m., soccer practice is less than an hour away, and Nat's out in his sandbox, where he's breaking in his birthday excavating equipment.

Mom forms a quick battle plan. *Got to remember the instructor's advice about how to handle Nat's blow-ups and his constant insistence on doing things his way.* (Have you guessed the two problem personality traits? You may want to review the list on page XX.) *When I ask him to do something, I'm supposed to start out with some support, maybe five minutes of playing with him. Then I give him a five-minute egg-timer warning. When the buzzer goes off and he doesn't stop his play, I'm supposed to count to three, and if he leaves without a fight he gets a lollipop. Still bothers me, this reward business. Why can't Nat just obey like other kids? But the reward's only for a couple of weeks until the situation improves. Got to have the sucker there with me; where is it? If he fights me, I'll carry him into the house and I can't say a word. Sounded good during the lesson. Hope I can remember it all.*

Nat and Mom have tried this routine several times with more failures than successes, mostly because Mom lost her temper and did way too much talking.

Mom approaches Nat, sits down in the sandbox, and smiles. "Wow, Nat. I didn't think that shovel tractor could hold that much sand."

Nat grins ear to ear; he's always such a happy fellow and he really enjoys playing. "Yeah, Mom. Look at the really big pile of sand I made."

Mom and Nat play and talk for several minutes. Then Mom eases into the bad news. "I know this is so much fun, but what did I say about soccer practice this morning?"

Nate's voice revs up. "Mom, I'm playing. I'm not going to stupid soccer."

Mom lets him talk without interrupting him. Then she sets the limits, while showing Nat the lollipop. "I'll set the timer for five minutes. And then you can choose to come nicely and get a sucker—"

"No, I'm not."

Mom sets the timer and walks away. After the timer goes off, she approaches Nat, counts to three, and Nat starts yelling again. Mom picks him up.

He immediately stops and says, "Mom, I'll stop! I want the lollipop."

Mom remembers the instructor's words: *If he yells but stops immediately when you pick him up, go ahead and give the reward. After several of these successful experiences, warn him that the requirement will be* no yelling *for the next lollipop.*

Mom gives him the lollipop. Nat gets dressed, keeping the lollipop within close reach (he can't unwrap it until he's in the car). In the car, he tilts his head, flashes his dimples, and says sweetly, "Mom, thanks for the lollipop."

Mom breaks into a smile, grateful for a successful exchange with her son. "You're welcome, buddy. Thanks for trying so hard to do what Mommy asks you to do."

Mom thinks, *Finally, it worked. This is more complicated than my consult with those Boeing engineers last week in Seattle. Sure beats yelling and feeling like a failure. The instructor said we've got a child with very intense reactions and off-the-charts persistence, and it's our job to harness these potentially good traits—now. Whew, I think we've finally got the ball rolling in the right direction.*

How do you like how Mom harnessed Nat's INTENSITY OF REACTION and his PERSISTENCE? Some of this behavior is age appropriate for a four-year-old child, but Nat's behavior is over the top. Mom's done a lot of good prep work. She expects Nat's reaction and has attuned her discipline to fit his personality traits. Consistent, firm, well-prepared consequences are always important, but they're especially critical with Nat's personality. When these traits are successfully managed, all kinds of good things happen. Who knows? He may be the next CEO for Caterpillar Equipment Company.

Attunement Checklist

The Shermans and Thomases are examples of how parents can attune their parenting approach to their children's personality traits. Here's a quick attunement checklist to help you implement these strategies into your own family life:

- Use the list in this chapter to identify your child's problem personality traits. And while you're at it, identify your own. A lot of parenting frustration is caused by parent-child personalities that are different. For example, you may be a more intense person while your daughter is extremely cautious. But with attunement, frustration will be significantly decreased.

- Be proactive in acknowledging your child's positive traits on a regular basis.

- Accept your child's inborn personality traits—the good ones as well as the to-be-improved ones. Acceptance achieves two critical outcomes: You'll stop trying to orchestrate a complete makeover, and your child will feel more accepted. Work toward noticeable trait improvement, but don't expect the problem trait to go away completely.

- Adjust your expectations for trait improvement until the behavior gets better. If the behavior doesn't change, lower your expectations more. With your intense child, allow a raised voice but with "I" statements, such as "I'm upset," instead of "Leave me alone." Once this step is solidly in place, go to the next step: Require a calmer voice while your child says the I statement. Don't increase expectations too fast.

- Be sure you are daily yielded to the guidance and power of God's Spirit, who fills you with love, peace, patience, gentleness, and self-control—especially in life's tough situations—if you let Him.

Being accepted and having his or her personality understood is the way every child wants to be treated. We've just witnessed the Golden Rule's answer for pulling off this important need for attunement. The benefits are huge, and your child's deep-down motivation to please you and become a better person is turbo-charged. You can expect great results.

Now we're ready for another Golden Rule parenting gem: how to maximize your child's successes and transform failures into positive experiences to help him or her become a better person. All children love successes and want failures to be handled in a positive way; it's the way we all would like to be treated. Mixing the two together is a bit tricky, but in the next chapter you'll learn just the right combination for you and your child.

CHAPTER 5

"Please Enhance My Chances of Success"

AMONG EVEN THE BEST-intentioned of us, the relational part of life—our family and friends—often gets short-changed in lieu of the pursuit of professional achievement or personal gain. Few people are able to pull off the balancing act required for both relational and personal success. But with the Golden Rule approach, this balancing act can become an ongoing, satisfying habit.

When we stop to think about it, we have to admit that searching for success really dominates every daily hour. Starting the day with your favorite cup of coffee gives you that cherished moment of bliss. Losing those last ten pounds will really make you happy. What about finally getting that fifty-two-inch 3D HDTV? You'll really feel great if you pull off your New Year's resolution: two date nights a month with your wife and one-to-one time with your child twice a week. The list of what we want in order to acquire happiness is endless, and over time it tends to get longer.

I call this list our "success beliefs," things we seek to acquire or complete or fulfill because we know doing so will make us happy. Some successes are short-lived, others long- term; some are destructive, some constructive.

Have you ever done a complete success beliefs inventory? Most of us have not. Given our Golden Rule approach, we need to take a quick snapshot of our success beliefs to see how we would really like to treat ourselves in order to feel truly successful. I challenge you to try this: On a sheet of paper or on your computer screen, write the phrase *I will be happy when . . .*Then list what you feel needs to happen in order for you to feel true happiness.

You might be surprised at what comes to mind.

Most of us automatically teach our success beliefs to our children in a "what's good for the goose is good for the gander" sort of way. In this chapter, however, we need to downshift and maybe even head in a different direction to help your child find *his* or *her* healthy success beliefs and the best ways to achieve them. Which success beliefs are best for your child and how do you teach them?

What Are the Healthiest Successes?

As Ryan's soccer team gathers up their gear and the players jump around like bouncing ping-pong balls giving high fives, Coach Jim takes Ryan's dad aside and says, "You know, next year Ryan will be eligible for the eight-to-ten-year-old bracket in the new Fire Storms team. It's by invitation only, but I'll get right to the point. I'm formally inviting Ryan to the team. Practice starts in September, which gives him a week or so to rest. Instead of three practices a week, it'll be four. It's a four-month season with six out-of-town games a year. Isn't this going to be an incredible opportunity for Ryan?"

Dad's eyebrows raise and he catches his breath, trying to act calm. "Well . . . thanks, Jim. We'll need to know a lot more about it, but I think Ryan will be thrilled. This upcoming soccer season will be Ryan's fifth year playing. I can hardly get to any of his games the way it is. We'll get back to you."

On the way home, between gulps of his juice box, Ryan asks, "Hey, Dad, what was Coach Jim asking?"

"He invited you to be a member of the Fire Storms starting in a month. It's really an honor. That's the best team in town."

Silence.

Dad darts a fast glance at Ryan, who is staring out the window. "Don't you think it's a big deal?"

Ryan thinks, *I'm so tired. I was looking forward to no soccer for at least two months. I've got to tell Dad something.* "Yeah . . . uh . . . Dad, I guess it'd be fun. Can we stop at McDonald's?"

Dad thinks, *I can't believe he's not more excited.* Several other thoughts race through his mind, including his wife's cautionary warning: "Don't be too pushy. Ryan may not be the next—"

"Dad, there's McDonald's."

"Oh, yeah, let's go." Dad's voice is barely audible.

Ryan glances at Dad. *Yikes! He's frowning. Okay, I'll sign up. It means so much to Dad, and I've got to act interested.*

Does this sound familiar? Great achievement feels *so* good for everyone, and it also brings anticipation of future happy successes. No wonder achievement dominates our lives, particularly in sports and academics. The life lessons learned in sports are priceless: hard work gets great results, there's no "I" in *team*, exercise is essential for good mental and physical health, there are benefits of both winning and losing, and self-confidence can grow quickly.

But there's another side to the success coin: pleasing a parent at the expense of not knowing enough about "my own needs" and not having enough free time for fun and relationships (both friends and family). It's really hard not to get carried away as a parent when your child is a high achiever in sports, one of society's two crown jewels of success (academic achievement is the other).

Dad's got a decision to make: Should Ryan play for the Fire Storms? Here are several quick tips for Dad to consider:

- Don't tamper with your child's initial ideas as he or she attempts to reach a decision. You've got to discipline yourself to listen. Remember, children want to be good and please you (chapter 3). If you talk first and don't start where your child is (chapter 2), your child's feelings and decisions will be influenced too much by your opinion. Put your thoughts aside—I know that's next to impossible when we're talking about success—and listen when your child answers your questions. Remember, always mix in more of your child's ideas than yours when helping your child establish his or her success beliefs.

- Learn your child's passion and focus on best efforts, not just end results. Maybe soccer is Ryan's main passion, and maybe Fire Storms is the best choice. When establishing the best-effort habit, don't go too far. Doing so can lead to burnout or workaholism. Start encouraging your child's best efforts by two years of age to establish a solid work habit. Your child will need a lot of assistance to finish a job at first, and when you say, "Let's pick up your toys together," you're demonstrating your commitment to the task but, even more, your commitment to your child. Remember to mix hard work with fun and play with others (more on this relational aspect later).

Whew! Time for a break. Those quick tips sure look good on paper, but maybe you're feeling overwhelmed by all the "to dos" when you're already scheduled to the hilt. Maybe this will help: Don't think overnight success; think long-term success. You'll want to start when your child is around two years old and chip away at it daily until your child reaches eighteen. You'll try it, apply it, and modify it over and over. The most enduring, satisfying successes take months and years to realize.

Hey, Kids!

Hey, kids, how do you like the point of considering your ideas when it comes to decisions? Every kid I've counseled complains, "Mom and Dad don't understand me." You're right. Parents often forget to listen because they have so many important things to teach you. If you're like the kids I talk to, you feel happy when your parents take your ideas seriously. And what about the hard work stuff? It's just natural to fight it. Everyone wants to do what's fun now, and with hard work, the fun is usually at the end. It's great to finish stuff, though, and when you do a good job you feel a lot of self-satisfaction. Here's what I want to you think about. When Dad asks you to work on something, even if it's boring, consider just doing it and not complaining. Even the Bible weighs in on this get-along strategy by saying, "Children, obey your parents . . . for this is right" and "Honor your father and your mother" (see Ephesians 6:1 and Exodus 20:12). Although it may not feel fun at times, honoring and obeying Mom and Dad is a *huge* part of becoming a successful person.

Let's look for a moment at the other societal success crown jewel, academic achievement. Haley's just finished her first month as a high school freshman. She's having a blast, but her parents are not completely happy with the direction she's headed.

Mom's just finished doing a computer check on Haley and, true to form, grades have slid from Bs to Cs and even one D. Last week there were two missing assignments, though Haley said all of her work had been handed in. But the socialization department is going great guns. She's got several good long-term friends, she's texting, Skyping, and tweeting all the time, and there's a junior—the school's star quarterback—who wants to "go out" with her. And to complicate matters, he's telling Haley it's old-fashioned to go on group dates.

Mom shares her concern with Dad: "On this dating deal, I vote for sticking with our group-dates-only rule. And we've got to put our foot down on her schoolwork. She doesn't have a learning disability; we've ruled that out. She's just such a social butterfly. This happens every year about this time. Her grades start dropping, and by the end of the quarter we'll probably have more Cs and Ds. Will you talk with her?"

Dad's mind races. *As far as I'm concerned, she can only group date until she's eighteen. But school stuff? My folks always insisted on As and Bs. I always delivered, barely, but I was miserable. I hated school. I swore I'd never do that to—*

"Ted, I asked you a question. Will you talk with her? I know your folks bugged the heck out of you and you don't want that for Haley. But we've got to do something."

Ted shoves his memories aside and makes a suggestion. "Let's get our notes out from that class we took last month on raising a successful teen."

Mom agrees. They went over the summary section that outlined three aspects of teen success: (1) establish close, healthy relationships (peer and family); (2) establish solid work behavior according to the child's capacity with sports, academics, and so forth; (3) establish and maintain good character qualities (trustworthy, respectful, hardworking, independent, humble, caring, positive attitude).

Mom makes a suggestion: "Let's both grade Haley on these three success aspects."

To their surprise they both come up with the same grades.

- Relationships: A (Dad's margin note: "I vote for an all-girls school.")

- Academic effort: D

- Character: C+ (Trustworthy on everything but telling the truth about missing homework. Not hard-working at school, but she does stick to the end with other stuff, loves working with special-needs kids, very independent, not so humble, but always a positive attitude.)

They decide on what they'll tackle: Insist on Haley's best academic effort and along with it two character traits—trustworthiness and hard work. Their teen success instructor said strict discipline was needed to establish the habit of hard work. Before, Mom and Dad had relied on lecturing—mostly endless reminding—which usually ended in a yelling match and everyone feeling like a failure.

So here's the plan Mom and Dad came up with. They decided Haley would have no phone usage—including texting, of course—until she had at least Bs on all her homework for two straight weeks along with no missing homework for the same period. And no screen time until her homework was completed, verified by showing her parents the work was done. And if there were any disrespectful comments, no screen time for that evening.

Mom and Dad almost never made waves with Haley, so you can imagine their uneasiness when their instructor advised they'd have to hunker down for a tsunami immediately after they delivered their ultimatum. And sure enough, when Haley was informed of the plan, you'd think the world had come to an end. She threw the biggest fit ever.

Mom and Dad tried as hard as they could to follow the instructor's guidelines: Seek the highest ground possible, weather the storm for at least two weeks, and don't even think of taking your warden hat off. He said negotiation in this type of situation is a signal to a teen to open the floodgates.

After a week of getting their feet wet with this new approach, everything settled down, and three weeks later Haley had her phone back. There were a few relapses, but Mom and Dad kept their warden hats on and the relapses were short lived. The instructor assured them that relapses were normal and provided an opportunity to establish that *We mean business.*

Haley's parents didn't know it, but they were helping to develop a lot of good things in Haley with their efforts. They were successfully teaching two character traits—hard work and trustworthiness—and how hard work is always satisfying even if the result isn't what you wanted. There's still the self-satisfaction of *I did my best.*

Hey, Kids!

Kids, don't you just hate it when your excuses don't keep your mom or dad from bugging you about a problem that never goes away? You know, cleaning your room or picking up your messes. But did you notice that if you keep failing, you feel pretty crummy and it gets tough to find a way out of the mess? Try to remember this: If something doesn't work, don't keep doing it over and over again! When Mom or Dad tries something new, don't fight it so much. Try harder, and it'll probably help you succeed and be a lot happier. That's a good thing.

That's it for the "what" part of success. By now you've learned something about the three main success beliefs to teach your child. You want your child to (1) establish close relationships with family and peers; (2) through hard work, achieve at the highest level possible according to his or her capacity with plenty of time for play; and (3) establish good character traits. Now let's take a closer look at several critical "how to's" in the next several pages before we close this chapter.

How to Make Your Child Successful

At a recent outdoor holiday event I saw a guy juggling five tennis balls. He even continued juggling while he carried on a conversation with a six year old. Then a gust of wind came up, and all the tennis balls hit the ground. He laughed, picked them up, and went at it again. I saw at least four success lessons in that two-minute event: (1) a close relationship is vital for success to occur (the juggler had a close relationship between the tennis balls and himself—he knew exactly how the tennis balls would respond to his actions); (2) focused effort leads to remarkable success; (3) accepting failure with a smile is part of success; and (4) for the best chance of success, many parts of an activity need to be in sync at the same time.

Helping your child learn to be successful really is a juggling act of the highest order for everyone. Do you recognize the Golden Rule in all of the above lessons? Let me help.

- Relationship: We all want a good, understanding relationship with our children. The need never goes away, and requires our full attention. It's the foundational requirement for teaching your child success beliefs.

- Best effort: We resist the discipline that effort takes at the beginning of a learning curve, but we love the results of disciplined effort, so almost everyone eventually accepts disciplined effort as necessary for the good life.

- Failure: We want to be comfortable with failure instead of feeling ashamed.

- Syncing all parts: We all want the parts of an activity to work together well.

So, settle in and let's take a look at some reality TV clips about how this all works.

The bell rings. *TGIF!* Isabella quickly stuffs her school things into her backpack. She wants to be at the curb when Dad's new blue Raptor pickup pulls up. She tries to walk as fast as she can without running and thinks, *Fourth grade's really been hard, especially math. I feel so dumb sometimes. Dad says it's no big deal. "We'll work it out," he says. I don't see how, but ... Can't wait to play softball with Dad at our Friday time together. It's so much— Hey! There's Dad!*

Big smile. Big wave. She bounces into the truck. Dad reaches out for the big hug and says, "How's my princess Bella, the belle of the ball?"

Dad's so funny. He made my name into Bella, belle of the ball. Silly Dad!

Nothing but party time to the park, at the park, and on the way home.

Fast forward to homework time right after dinner. First Isabella gets all her chores done, making sure she puts all her dishes in the dishwasher and cleans off the table. Then she picks up her room, thinking, *Mom and Dad said it's nice to have things cleaned up for the weekend. I don't see why, but that's the rules.* Isabella fought all her chores at first, but her folks wouldn't budge and eventually the chores became a habit. At the beginning she argued a lot, but her parents put a stop to that by sending her to her room when she gave her opinion disrespectfully or didn't do the job "according to specs."

Later, Isabella sits down at the kitchen table with Mom, opens her math book, and looks at her mom, fighting back the tears. "I got a D today on my math quiz, and I really studied hard. I know you said I don't need to feel stupid, but the teacher said only three students got Ds. What's wrong with me?"

Mom touches Isabella's shoulder and says warmly, "Everyone has things they're good at. Your reading is at the seventh-grade level, remember? And everyone struggles with some things. For you, it's math—at least right now. It's the way we're made. Chemistry was really hard for your dad. Did you know he thought he was dumb as a teenager because his chemistry grades in high school were Cs and Ds?"

Isabella straightens up and yells at Dad in the other room, "Dad, is that true?"

Dad comes in and tells Isabella all the gory details, and Isabella hangs on every word.

Then Dad says, "When I was a junior, my dad got me a computer for Christmas. I couldn't believe how fun it was. I started taking computer classes and got straight A's. I couldn't believe school could be so much fun. That's why I love my computer job at HP. I found what I love to do."

Mom and Dad start talking about how to solve the math problem in Isabella's homework. Isabella feels better again, thinking, *I guess math just isn't my strength, whatever that means. I'm still—*

Dad interrupts her thoughts. "Bella, what do you think of getting a tutor?"

"Dad, it'll be boring." She thinks for a minute, and then in a sing-song way says, "Okay, I guess I'll try."

Dad looks at Mom, smiles, and says, "Mom and I have talked. We're going to reduce your math homework 50 percent so you can be successful. Your teacher said success is really important when we're first working our way out of a sticky problem. Latter on when you're feeling better about things, maybe you can do the whole assignment."

Isabella squirms and says quietly, "But I don't want to be different than the other kids." She thinks for a moment and then says, "But it sure would feel good for math not to be so hard. Let's try it for a few weeks."

Do you hear the Golden Rule approach in these conversations? There's a good relationship that's been built on understanding and acceptance, wanting to be good, starting *where I am*, and developing good character traits—hard work, mutual respect, independence (doing all the chores herself). And when all these important parts are synced together, failure gets reframed as an opportunity for understanding and growth rather than feeling *I'm bad*. Helping kids (and adults) feel *I'm good* when dealing with a failure? No wonder the Golden Rule has endured for centuries!

Are you thinking, *Yeah, sure. Who has a Brady Bunch family, an easy kid, and an involved dad?* It's almost unheard of. You're right. But keep trying this parenting approach, and I think you'll be surprised at how familiar the Brady Bunch will seem to you.

Let's dig a little deeper and cement two more key points into place.

First, as you read in the previous chapter, experts report that 40 percent of us have an easy kid, and the rest of us have more-difficult kids. Over and over again I've seen the whole range of easy-to-dif-ficult children improve noticeably with this Golden Rule approach. Keep trying; you'll be successful.

Second, and perhaps one of the most important, points, note Dad's involvement. Dad, it's true; you're often are not involved enough. (Don't stop reading; I'm a dad and I've got your back.) Whether dads are in the home or not, all kinds of good things happen when they're more involved. Kids experience fewer behavior problems (and are more likely to delay sexual activity and avoid drugs), better aca-demic achievement, and good relationships as adults. Hands down, involved dads help children establish healthy success beliefs.

So, Dad, let's talk man-to-man for a moment. There are reasons why you may not be as involved as would be healthy for your child.

- Most dads had a disengaged dad themselves. Father skills are learned; we're not born with them. Unfortunately, most dads reading this book had disengaged dads, either due to a divorce or because their dads simply did not spend much time with them. Kid translation: *I'm not worth much.*

- Dads often feel their opinions are not respected by moms. It's human nature to withdraw when we don't feel respected. And in defense of moms, a dad's parenting style can reflect a disengaged dad's approach. Often it's too harsh and delivered with variations of the old-fashioned "children should be seen and not heard." But there is a big silver lining. Dad's harshness, toned down a bit, can be transformed into consistent, firm limit-setting—a critical child-rearing requirement. Moms sometimes don't pull off this firm approach adequately because they're more focused on lov-ing and nurturing. Mixing firmness with nurturing is tricky, but with practice it can be done.

- Dads often are solution based. Solutions are critical, but that's the parenting tip above the iceberg. The best solutions occur as a re-sult of adequate understanding and nurturing. Sometimes moms exclude dads who are mostly solution oriented. Mix understanding and solution skills together just right and you may get an Oprah interview.

Sound a little farfetched? It's not. Here's my recommendation based upon my personal experience raising four children, coupled with more than forty years of helping dads get more engaged:

- Your solution-based, "Do as I say" approach is really valuable, as long as you're willing to learn the understanding and acceptance skills before you put your foot down. Being firm and consistent is crucial, but not all that successful as a stand-alone skill.

- Find a parenting class where both you and your partner can learn mutually agreed-upon parenting skills. When you're both pulling in the same direction, you'll dramatically increase your likelihood of success.

- Develop as close a relationship as possible with your partner. Experts say kids in this type of family flourish: They behave better, get better grades, and are more successful as adults (in work and relationships). Besides, there are two huge benefits for you: You'll enjoy parenting more, and your romantic life will improve tenfold. I recommend periodic marital workshops or short-term marital counseling to jumpstart your efforts and keep your successes at the highest level possible.

Please don't close the book; hear me out on this point about seeking assistance. The ability to get along with someone every day for several years, especially when the differences are enormous, is not a skill that comes naturally to most of us. Really, it's a wonder the divorce rate is as low as it is. Wouldn't you ask for help in your job if you were struggling? (If you didn't, a good supervisor would get you the help you needed, whether you wanted it or not.) Same thing with marriage. Consider improving your marital relationship skills with a competent counselor. Do it and you'll look forward to coming home.

So we've examined the Golden Rule approach to happy successes. It's all about discovering the most meaningful "wants" and the healthiest steps to get there. The Golden Rule gets to the bottom line—everyone feels successful when they are treated with understanding and acceptance. And there's a ticket to get there: Discipline your child to establish enduring relationships and good character, along with the right amount of achievement and material things. That's a recipe for a truly successful life.

CHAPTER 6

"I Need for Us to Agree to Disagree Agreeably"

"YOU'RE WRONG."

Dead silence from all ten special-education staff members—except for the deafening "You're wrong" reverberating against every wall like a Chinese gong. A well-respected counselor had just given an ADHD diagnosis to the student being staffed into the program. And then came the booming voice of the head school psychologist: "You're wrong."

While everyone fumbled with pens or papers, the team leader finally gathered her wits and haltingly said, "Let's, uh, let's take a ten-minute break." Everyone made a beeline for the closest door.

In the hallway three teachers circled the counselor, and one teacher made this muffled, from-the-heart comment: "I'm sorry for the unprofessional response."

The "guilty" counselor quietly responded with a half-smile. "You know, some people get really emotional when they disagree with someone, especially when it comes to diagnosing ADHD kids. Everyone's got their way of correcting another person."

One teacher leaned forward as if she were preparing to share a well-kept secret, eyes darting to her fellow teachers, then whispering in an agitated voice to the counselor, "How can you be so self-assured? I feel like someone just stabbed me. No one should be treated that way." Tears welled up in her eyes.

We've all been in situations like this; we've dished it out and we've received it, and we know it can get ugly fast. Truth be known, it doesn't matter who we are—even if we're well-educated, well-trained professionals—all of us fumble through situations in which we're accused of being wrong or we feel others are wrong. Every day, we're given opportunities to build up healthy calluses or find ourselves in a world of hurt.

Being wrong usually hurts, but it doesn't need to be excruciating if the right training is done in the home. And that's where training opportunities abound. Rachael doesn't pick up her room, Nathan lies, Jamie yells. Dad misses his quarterly report deadline, and Mom completely forgets her brother-in-law's birthday. Wrong, wrong, wrong. Making wrong right, in the right way, is what you'll learn by the end of this chapter.

Let's put the Golden Rule to work and ask a now-familiar question: When you're wrong, how would you like to be treated: "You're wrong and you should be ashamed of yourself," or "That's unacceptable behavior and it needs to stop; let's fix it together"? Of course, the agreeable, positive approach is much more satisfying. It's really not necessary to keep poking at an open sore. But some discomfort is necessary to motivate change. Mixing in just the right degree of discomfort is another thing you'll learn to do in the following paragraphs.

What makes correcting a mistake so tough to do in the right way? Because, deep inside, we parents want things our way, right now. James 4:1 says, "What causes fights and quarrels among you? Don't they come from your desires that battle within you?" Let's face it: Junior's getting under our skin. He deserves a good yell-at with a clear ultimatum attached. So we're naturally inclined to respond with high-volume, frustrated scoldings complete with put-downs and threats . . . those are the "desires that battle within" us when Junior crosses the boundaries.

Two key character qualities (or "fruit") of the Spirit are gentleness and self-control. We need to enlists these two qualities during difficult times.

This isn't to say that firmness, correction, and consequences are not appropriate—for indeed they are. The Bible is very clear about the need for parents to discipline their children. But it's also clear on doing so gently, in control of our emotions. Of not "exasperating" our children with unreasonable discipline. Of *agreeing to disagree agreeably.*

The human condition is like rich soil. Everyone knows it's got great potential, but it will grow weeds. A good gardener minimizes the weeds, maximizes the plant growth, and does so without causing significant damage. The gardener knows if she lets the weeds get out of hand, she will not get many of those tasty strawberries.

That's exactly what we all face every day: the task of continually weeding out negative behavior and doing everything possible to raise a good child without damaging his or her self-esteem. "Am I doing the right thing? Does my yelling damage my kid? How bad is it for my child that I'm a single parent?" Questions galore. Even though you've probably read several of the thousands of available parenting books, trying to do the right thing seems to keep our blood pressure on the high side.

Take a couple of deep breaths. I've found a way to keep the blood pressure in the 120/80 range—without medication or meditation. It's another Golden Rule gem: *Disagree agreeably and find a mutually agreeable solution whenever possible.* "Rachael, there's no choice [disagree] about picking up your room. Even though it's really boring, let's find a way [agreeable] to get it done before noon on Saturday without whining. You can choose to start Friday night before bed or Saturday before eleven o'clock." Here's a typical, mutually agreeable solution: Rachael picks Friday night and Mom sets the rules. She says, "You must start picking up your room by eight o'clock and be done by nine. If you're not done, there'll be no screen time on Saturday. And with her warden hat tilted just right, Mom imposes the consequence—*every time*—if the crime is committed (deadline not met).

You've already seen this "disagree agreeably" gem played out with Jared and his parents in chapter 2. I call it the "Discussion Procedure": state concerns first and mutual solutions second. This is not just another parenting technique, one that looks good on paper but doesn't fit your situation. This parenting shoe will fit your child to a T. My young clients consistently respond something like this when their parents use the Discussion Procedure: "When I mess up, my mom understands me and then she puts the pedal to the metal." Stress but no damage, bending but not breaking, when the child is disciplined.

Sounds so simple, but that's typical of the Golden Rule. Being understood when making mistakes is how all humans want to be treated, especially children.

So get your work clothes on, grab your gloves, and let's get on our hands and knees and learn how to "garden" your kid's heart. Interesting, isn't it, that you can't garden standing up. Takes a lot of humility to discipline our children when it comes to cultivating the heart.

Before we dig in, let's do a little prep work with a "quick and clean" (we'll get dirty soon enough) review of what we've learned so far. Then we'll get to work tending to your child's four "heart parts" and using some really effective tools to get the job done.

All the Golden Rule material we've covered has an "agreeable" orientation. *Understand* your child by validating thoughts and feelings before dealing with behavior. *Start where your child is* (personality, developmental aspects). *Focus* on your child's "I want to be good" motivation to the hilt. *Make sure* "family and friend successes" take center stage. I don't know about you, but my heart warms up when I hear these points. I wonder if the FDA would consider these nitty-gritty agreeability guidelines as the best "emotional heart diet" equivalent to their pyramid "high fiber, low-fat" diet.

Tending the Heart's Four Parts

In one of my workshops on discipline, a parent and her middle-school son, Nathan, graciously volunteered to be interviewed about a lying problem. Let's watch the video clip, but a heads up. You'll need your headset to hear Nathan's heart thoughts as he listens to and talks with his mother. We'll learn firsthand all about the heart's four parts.

Before we listen in, let's find out how Nathan's lying got started. Nathan's never been a go-getter (AVOIDANCE personality; see chapter 2), and he's always resisted chores and homework. He never wants to do things now, always saying, "I'll do it in a little bit." In the last year Nathan's lying has increased and he's getting downright defiant. When Mom asks him if he's finished his homework, he scowls and says, "I already did it," or "Quit bugging me." And Mom's gotten into the habit of saying, "I've told you five times already. . . ." And her yelling is not good for her voice or Nathan's ears.

So here's the video of the session.

Mom begins talking while Nathan does a visual of my office. "Nathan's really a good kid—he doesn't cause trouble at school, he's good with his sister—but he can't tell me the truth about stuff. He even lies about brushing his teeth."

Nathan's thinking, *Yeah, butter me up, Mom. You never tell me the good stuff unless you're trying to impress another adult. You're not fooling me, and I bet you're not going to tell this dude about how you're always yelling at me. . . . Great . . . Thanks for telling him about the teeth-brushing thing.*

Mom throws up her hands while glancing at Nathan. Then she turns to me. "It's so silly. He'll tell me he brushed his teeth, and I show him the brush isn't even wet." Now her face clouds over as she tilts forward in her seat, trying to make eye contact with Nathan. (We can hear Nathan thinking, *Brace yourself, here it comes, look calm.*) "Nathan Edward, look at me. Isn't that right Nate?"

Nathan's thoughts race as he shifts into backtalk mode: *Brushing my teeth is so boring . . . used to be she'd believe me . . . this is embarrassing being in front of this guy, having him hear my mom's putdowns . . . .* Then Nathan says, "I do too brush my teeth. The brush just gets dry before you check it." His voice reaches a high-pitched whine as he says, "Besides, you're always yelling at me for no reason."

Tears well up in his eyes as I hand him the tissue box. He pushes the box away, blinking, trying desperately to shut out the tears, and says, "Thanks, I've just got allergies today."

Mom shakes her head ever so slightly in disapproval, eyes rolling like those of an astronaut in an antigravity chamber.

Nathan sees it and thinks, *She can't make me cry. I'm not going to do it.* He looks away from us, blinks hard, and catches a glimpse of the Lego creation on my coffee table. He says in a sing-song tone as he looks deep into my eyes, "I made a space vehicle like that." Mom starts to comment, but I give her a gentle "stop" hand signal while I lean forward, smile, and say, "Tell me what it looks like."

The creation he describes is amazing.

He's thinking, *It's fun to talk about fun stuff and have an adult know what's fun. Wish Dad paid attention to my Star Wars Lego fleet.*

Does any of this sound familiar? Important things are not getting done, you've tried everything in the books, but, flop, you're dead in the water. And your child doesn't ever connect the dots even when you point them out: "I wouldn't yell if you just did what I asked you to do. And what I ask is so basic; I'm not asking you to design the next Mars manned spacecraft. I just want you to pick up your dirty clothes!" And Mom's feeling downright terrified deep inside: *Am I raising a lying sociopath?*

As you read the story, are you wondering why children lie? Here's why: *They can't stand to make their parents unhappy.* When asked to tell the truth and they know the truth will be "prison," two thoughts flash through their minds: (1) *If I don't tell the truth, I won't disappoint my parents,* and (2) *30 percent of the time my parents don't find out the truth. Maybe this time will be one of the 30 percenters.* Those are the two things I eventually hear from every child who lies regularly.

I know this doesn't make sense from the above-ground, logical perspective. But lying does make sense—sounds weird, I know—

from the down-deep, *I'm always wrong*, heart perspective. Always remember, the first answers to problem solving come from the heart (often unconscious). This lying problem gets resolved when you start with tending to the heart instead of the head-shrinking lectures.

Back to Mom's head-shrinking response. Haven't we all been there? Maybe that's where you are now. So what do we do first? We do an emotional EKG of the four critical heart parts: softness, rightness, "worthness," "growthness." (Those last two words are Unruh and not Webster, but I think you'll soon see how they get at two really important parts of the heart.) Here are Nathan's test results complete with the following sections: *reading, recommendation*, and *fix-it tools*.

1. Softness

Reading: Significant hardening (surface reading only); fertile (deep core)

Recommendation: The more Nathan believes he's being heard, the more he will feel hope—a sure sign that the fertile, deep core is being cultivated and will eventually surface. Hardened hearts result in stunted growth (both emotionally and physically) and a lot of unhappiness.

Fix-it tool: Listening (Discussion Procedure, concerns step, part 1)

- Child talks, you listen (no interruptions).
- You repeat what your child says, finishing by saying, "Did I get everything you said?" (Repeat until you've correctly heard everything. "Mute" your points.)
- You talk and your child listens. (Train your child not to interrupt.)
- Your child repeats. (Begin this process when your child is as young as two years old.)

2. Rightness

Reading: 90 percent wrong daily

Recommendation: Mom needs to immediately agree with something Nathan says when she's beginning to correct a wrong behavior such as lying. (*Do not* discipline yet; only after agreement has sunk in.) Nathan needs logical, head-type words that touch his heart. Agreement is the combination needed to unlock the heart. Here's a sample agreement statement: "I agree, chores are really boring and you hate school. Tell me what's so awful about it and we'll do everything possible to make it interesting without me always yelling at you. That way you might not need to lie so much."

Warning: Humans routinely make five negative comments for every one positive comment, both to themselves and others. The physical and emotional results are equivalent to a high-fat diet. Go "lite" on the negatives (25 percent) and heavy on the positives (75 percent).

Fix-it tool: Agreement (Discussion Procedure: concerns step, part 2—do not require this from your child until his or her early teen years)

- Right after you have listened and repeated his or her statement (see the "listening" tool above), agree with something your child has said. For example, "You do really enjoy drawing; you should be upset that you can't stay up later," or "That X-box Live game is so fun, especially when you've qualified as the squadron leader. You're learning a lot about teamwork." (Did you know that adults who played team-related video games in their younger years make better team members as adults?)

- Start to introduce your disagreement : "I understand it's fun, but there's too much violence in the game." (Don't get into your limit-setting consequences yet; that's reserved for the mutual problem-solving tool you'll see in the Growthness section of this report. "Easy as she goes" is a good motto to follow when change is involved.)

Let's take a break for a minute from the report and point out how good agreement feels. It opens up the *I'm right* tributaries; the self-worth reservoir gets filled to the point that self-improvement can happen more easily even during the storms of problem solving. We can weather the storms of problem solving so much better when we start with a self-assured foundation. The human engine of *I want to be good* fires up and great things start to happen.

Does the idea of "I'm-right tributaries" sound confusing? As I've pointed out before, when children do something wrong, their inside heart-talk shifts into black-and-white mode (I've heard it from *every one* of my clients). *I'm right* or *I'm wrong* means *I'm good* or *I'm bad*. And *I'm bad* doesn't mean just *my behavior's bad*; it means *I'm bad—all of me*. Our agreement tool neutralizes this harmful response: *What I did needs to be changed, but it doesn't mean I'm a bad person*. This allows growth to flourish!

One brief, really important clarification about this I'm bad business. Some stress or discomfort is critical for change to happen. You *want* your child to feel some stress, but only as deep as the behavior goes. You want him or her to understand that lying will not be tolerated. But don't let the stress sink into the core of your child. Communicate along this line: "I'm understanding why you lie; let's find a way for you to feel safe telling me when you do something wrong." Bottom line: Target your stress laser mostly on the surface behavior, not at the core of your child's heart.

You can see that this agreement tool engages heart talk. Your initial agreement words, at the start of a problem, are received as *I'm okay* and *I need to improve*. Now the problem is an opportunity for improvement, not further proof that *I'm damaged goods*.

One more quick side note before we cover the Worthness report. Did you know this "opportunity for improvement" phase is straight from the Honda assembly line? Way back in the mid-1940s, the Japanese found a way to turn mistakes into "opportunities for improvement." That phrase sure sounds more agreeable than "How could you have made such a dumb mistake?" And it keeps you from thinking, *Am I in big-time trouble now?* If it worked for Honda, it's got to have some benefits for human growth.

3. Worthness

Reading: ("red light" flashing) highly dangerous, requires immediate attention. Nathan believes nobody cares and he believes he's dangerously close to being totally worthless.

Recommendation: Immediately put yourself at the center of Nathan's heart and feel what he's feeling. Understand that Nathan's angry because he's fearful (potentially the most destructive of all emotions). Left unattended, expect more anger and increased hardening of the heart.

Fix-it tool: empathy

- Validate the heart with empathic "heart" words. Stay inside your child's heart and feel with him (keep your head out of it): "I'm sad that you're so fearful of displeasing me. When we're this scared, it's easy to make a decision to lie that ends up being wrong." I know this sounds like you're a $100-an-hour shrink, but with a little practice it will become natural. The pay's not that great, but the dividends are unending—far better than are anything you'll get from the stock market.
- Engage your child at this level for several minutes (remember, no disagreeing, only validating): "Tell me more about what you feel." Your taking feelings seriously makes your child trust you. When trust is in place, your child will take your direction really well.

This heart-to-heart empathy fix *will* maintain your child's heart in its original, soft condition. *I'm okay and need to continually im-*

prove is a really important foundation to establish from early on. Life's challenges are transformed into "opportunities for improvement." What an agreeable way to live.

4. Growthness

Reading: (Red light flashing again) previous tests in danger zone

Recommendation: Fix heart parts 1–3 immediately. Expect no growth until these parts are fixed. Then stimulate growth (self-improvement, problem-solving) through a mutually determined solution whenever possible. Don't all of us feel really good when an important person in our lives takes our ideas seriously, especially when we see our ideas are part of a solution? Feeling *I matter* really is an effective human growth fertilizer.

Fix-it tool: mutual solution

- Most of the time, the solution needs to contain the concerns voiced by both parent and child. For example, Nathan's mom might say, "Now I understand why you lie. You're afraid of my yelling and putting you down when you mess up, and I can see that I've done that" (acknowledging the child's concern). "What if I don't get upset when you admit you're wrong? And, for three weeks we'll have minimal consequences for what you did?" (solution based on both Mom's and Nathan's concerns). "Of course, if you steal again, you'll need to pay the money back."

- Some solutions (the minority) are not discussable. "We decided what would happen if you were out past your curfew. No car for a week. No discussion." Or when big-ticket rules are broken: "Breaking curfew is a no-no. You're grounded for a week and you must write a one-page paper about why curfew is important. We'll discuss it after the paper is written." We're not born with self-control. Children learn it from parents, and there are definitely times when it's best learned with no "ands, buts, or whatevers."

Let's take a brief minute to summarize what we've learned from these heart tests.

1. *Softness*—Keep the heart pliable and enriched to deal with life's many challenges. If the ground is parched, your valuable parenting seeds will not take root. Your child believing you *will listen* guarantees a pliable heart.

2. *Rightness*—Deal with wrongness as an opportunities for improvement, not proof that your child is "bad." Make the heart right and the behavior wrong. Starting with *agreement* ensures *I'm okay*. The new behavior you're trying to instill will have a much better chance of becoming deeply rooted.

3. *Worthness*—Strive to show your child *you're worth a lot* more than 75 percent of the time. Positives are the heart's "miracle grow." It's proof that your child is okay. Too little crystal-clear caring will result in your child's heart sending out a *why try?* message to the brain. If it happens too much, a child will start believing *I don't care*. Not a good thing. *Empathy*—you being at the center of your child's heart—during tough times proves *I'm worth a lot*.

   Warning: Don't make everything your child does the best thing since apple pie. Your child thrives on realistic feedback by focusing on his or her best efforts and behavior; "You sharing with your brother really made him feel good," or "You doing your chores without being asked really helps me out a lot." And when a wrong behavior occurs, don't water it down: "Not studying for tests isn't acceptable. Let's set up a one-hour study routine for test prep from now on." Then follow through.

4. *Growthness*—Make the Golden Rule win-win approach work regularly and you'll get vigorous growth. Finding *mutual solutions* results in this belief: "I know I'm understood by Mom and Dad because solutions to my problems usually fit what's best for me and almost always work." This approach turbo-

charges buy-in, and your child will end up at the high end of the psychological growth chart.

By the way, have you been looking at your own heart readings as we've been doing this testing? For most of us, the test results end up on the low side of the scale. Sad to say, but it's just not human nature to be agreeable with ourselves and others when wrong things happen.

But thank goodness the picture really brightens when you shine the Golden Rule light on your handling of mistakes. Through consistent cultivation of the heart, your child's budding and blossoming process is so satisfying.

Hey, Kids!

Kids, what do you think? When we first look at this agreement stuff, most kids tell me something like this: "Come on, this will never happen in my home." I answer, "I believe you, because that's what you feel. I know your parents need to do a better job listening to your thoughts, feelings, and concerns." (And I always add somewhere, "And you've got to do better at listening to your parents and doing what they say.")

Did you know that few adults know to use the tools described in this chapter? Most parents received very little training about how to work on agreement. Parents often think it's all supposed to come naturally, but it doesn't. Parenting's really super complicated. Your parents love you, but often it's hard to turn that love into "you're a really cool person." I know this is hard to believe, but your parents don't know everything.

Since your parents are reading this, they will get a lot better at this stuff. Try to be patient and make sure to tell them when you're upset, *respectfully.* And one more thing you've heard before: Do the boring things when you're told, and when you've messed up take the discipline without a lot of bellyaching comments. If you do, your remaining ten or so years at home will really be pretty decent. Hang in there.

Now we're ready to conclude this section of the book, "Now, Help Me Become a Better Person." When you first saw this title, perhaps you were thinking what most parents think: *Come on, really now? My kid fights me tooth and nail, but you're saying he wants to be a better person?* You're right. Kids typically resist behavior changes, and that makes parenting really tough.

Not so when the Golden Rule approach is implemented. It's provides a special light that illuminates in 3D Technicolor the heart's needs and how to transform those needs into appropriate behavior. That's the secret behind why children resist change so much—the heart is not engaged and tended to first. That's why a lot of parenting approaches don't quite get the job done; the head part is there, but the heart is mostly left out.

We've looked at some nitty-gritty parenting principles in this chapter. One of your child's biggest heart needs, especially when problems crops up, is to feel *I'm okay even though I need to correct what I did wrong.* And then we witnessed the Golden Rule's response to this seemingly impossible need: Find a way to agree with your child at the start of a problem and keep this agreeable approach going throughout the problem solving. I heard more than one "Aha!" along the way, as well. After all, who wouldn't want to be treated in this agreeable way? I hope this Golden Rule "agreeable" path is already making your parenting much more satisfying.

Before we leave this chapter, here's a last quick snapshot of the Golden Rule's "agree agreeably" approach.

The first surprise is that discipline starts with you not your child. You listen and don't talk—unless questions are asked—until you are inside your child's heart. Once inside, you don't discipline yet, you validate: "I can see why you cheated on your math test; you were so fearful of my reaction." Now you can discipline for appropriate behavior, as long as it fits your child's basic needs (personality traits, *start where I am*). "Let's get a math tutor so you can be more confident, and I promise not to make any more comments like 'How could you be so irresponsible to not study for that test.'" And then with a hug say, "If you're tempted to cheat, tell me and I will not be so upset, but I will not stop helping you until you break this habit."

The Golden Rule has one more hidden surprise to reveal: learning how to love and respect others. When you treat your child the way you want to be treated, your child will be inclined to treat others the way they've been treated by you. (Four "treats" in that last sentence; the Golden Rule sure is full of goodies.) But training is required. That's what week three's section is all about—teaching your child loving and respecting skills. I hope you'll be as satisfied as I've been when I see the results parents get when their children acquire these skills.

WEEK 3

"Now, Help Me Treat Others as I Want to Be Treated"

Helping Your Child Treat Others with Love and Respect

CHAPTER 7: "Please Help Me Respect Others"

CHAPTER 8: "Please Help Me Be Compassionate—
First with Myself"

CHAPTER 9: ". . . And Help Me Be Compassionate
with Others"

CHAPTER 10: "Please Help Me Learn Humility"

"Please Help Me Respect Others"

MOM AND DAD LOOK straight-faced at each other while exchanging unspoken thoughts as Ellie's sixth-grade teacher shuffles through her notes.

Mom thinks, *I can't believe Ellie had the gall to chew out her teacher in front of the whole class.*

Dad thinks, *It's finally happened . . . just like I thought it would: Ellie disrespecting her teacher just like she's been doing with us for the last six months. Embarrassing as—*

"Mr. and Mrs. Miller, I'm concerned about the disrespect your daughter shows me. The last straw was when she accused me—in front of the whole class, mind you—of being 'the worst teacher she'd ever had.' That was her response after I had just given her an after-school suspension for passing notes. And that was after I gave her two warnings."

This is just the first minute of what seems like an eternal, hour-long meeting. And all both Mom and Dad hear and feel is "Your daughter's messed up" and "You're screwed-up parents."

How high was your blood pressure as you felt the embarrassment along with these parents? As a consultant, I've been in hundreds of meetings like this one. The parents' pain is agonizing. Maybe you've never faced this type of situation, but every parent I've been around struggles with *wanting to make sure* they raise a respectful child, in part to avoid this type of situation.

How do you think Ellie ended up this way? Is she just a brat? Maybe she needs nothing less than a good tongue lashing and a weekend of bread and water and confinement to her room? Were Mom and Dad too lenient, a couple of those permissive parents who allowed too much backtalk, fearful of damaging her self-esteem if they put their foot down? What about the teacher's comment—"Ellie has a huge chip on her shoulder and can never admit being wrong"?

Where did Ellie's anger come from? Could it have anything to do with Dad being unemployed for a year and all the family stress and tension that's resulted from that tough circumstance?

Whew! Parenting sure gets tied up into multiple knots really fast, especially when disrespect starts to get out of hand. Teaching respect is really complicated, and it seems like parents need to be on it 25/8.

When we boil down the challenge, we're faced with this basic problem: Children are born with a normal, "my way or the highway," almost disrespectful orientation to living. You've got four years—birth to kindergarten—to help your child establish his or her basic ability for respectful behavior most of the time: *I don't like it, but I'll share my highway with you; just keep your distance.* And then you've got until eighteen years of age to establish a deeply rooted habit of respect.

Whether you've just started training your one-year-old or you're in a situation like the Miller family, there are clear-cut answers for teaching children to be respectful. And, as we've come to expect, the Golden Rule will serve as our primary guide to get the job done. Everyone likes to be treated with respect, and we all know how good it feels to be respected. And for extra motivation and guidance, we can keep in mind the incredibly powerful statement by the apostle Paul, who wrote that "the entire law [of God] is fulfilled in keeping this one command: 'Love your neighbor as yourself'" (Galatians 5:14). We're told in 1 Corinthians 13, the famous "love chapter" of the Bible, that love is patient and kind; it does not dishonor others and is not self-seeking. To love one's neighbor (or parent, or child, or sibling, or classmate, or friend, or foe) is to regard and treat that person with the same level of respect you want for yourself.

In this last section, we'll address three aspects of how to help your child treat others with the love and respect they want for themselves: (1) respect training, (2) caring for others and not forgetting to own "my part" of a problem, and (3) humility training.

Okay, enough warm-up; let's get started. Grab a beverage and settle into your favorite chair. Then take a look at this brief introduction of the show before we raise the curtain.

> Thank you for participating in our Golden Rule production—a remarkably simple, effective parenting approach. In this show you will again witness the Golden Rule's unique and simple approach: Become aware of how you would like to be treated (respected), then apply this information to your parenting. From the previous shows you have found out that everyone wants acceptance for who I am. And children thrive when we meet their need to be understood (personality, feelings) and that, when they feel understood, they'll want to learn from you how to be successful—especially if you teach them in an agreeable way.

> Your respectful acceptance of your child during the last several weeks has increasingly established self-respect within your child. Count on it, even if there is no direct evidence. The groundwork is now in place for respect training: establishing your child's skills to respect others.

> Enjoy the show.

The lights dim, the curtain opens, and we see four-year-old Ethan facing his dad. He tilts his head to one side, looks up at Dad, and says, "What's 'respect others' mean, Daddy?" (Where do they get these smart kids to act so perfectly? It's amazing.)

Here's what happened five minutes before this question. Ethan had just thrown five too many beans to Alphie and Dad followed through with the prearranged consequence: Remove Ethan from his chair. And as he did it, Ethan hit Dad's arm pretty hard and Dad said, "That's disrespectful and it hurts."

Now Ethan is calm after a brief timeout in his room and asking the "respect" question.

Dad says, "Come sit on Daddy's lap while we talk."

Ethan lights up and makes a perfect leap into his dad's lap.

Dad looks deep into Ethan's eyes and says, "You were really having fun with Alphie, and you got really upset when I wanted you to stop. And when kids are upset, they feel like hitting. But it hurts to get hit and it's not respecting me. It is respecting me to say 'I'm upset' instead of hitting."

Of course, as the therapist and writer, I can put all the healthy words in Dad's conversation to make sure everything's covered. It may sound like a pretty big stretch for you to talk like this with your child, but with practice you can get the points across in your own way—which is the best way anyway. The rewards are huge.

Ethan looks up at Dad, and with his typical creased-forehead, super-concentrating look, says, "Sorry, Daddy."

Dad kisses his forehead, they snuggle for a second, and Ethan looks up at his dad. His smile pops the dimples into place and they hug again.

All kids don't have a personality that lends itself to such a heartwarming exchange, but this scenario sure is full of Golden Rule "the way I'd like to be treated" qualities: plenty of understanding and acceptance sprinkled with validating words and physical warmth, as well as clear-cut discipline that involves firm limits. And Ethan's positive responsiveness—after the consequences were done—proves he was treated in the right way. (By the way, boys typically don't get as much physical warmth as girls—especially from dads—during the preschool years. Boys need it and thrive on it.)

And one last Golden Rule point before we continue. Children need and want (though you will not see it in their immediate actions) to be treated with firm limits when they go over the line, and limit setting needs to start in the early years. Self-control of thoughts and actions is a key respect requirement and important for a successful life. During the early years, the control comes from outside your child—from you. Make it constructive with clear, firm limits.

Speaking of your influence, your respectful responses toward yourself, loved ones, friends, co-workers, and especially your child are a critical part of your child's respect training. Children are sponges from birth. They feel and watch your every move and soak up every drop. Do you need to be perfect? Absolutely not. But if you follow the Golden Rule guidelines most of the time (try for at least 60 percent of the time) you'll be doing a great job as long as you keep your other responses as constructive as possible.

The rest of this chapter will cover three important aspects of respect training: (1) how parents show and tell respect; (2) establishing self-respect within your child; and (3) learning loving, respectful behaviors toward others.

How Parents Show and Tell Respect

A child's emotional heart is designed to soak up everything he or she feels, sees, and hears from you. That's what this section is about—you saturating your child with plenty of examples of healthy respect toward others and toward yourself.

You know your car runs a lot better if you take care of it: oil changes, periodic maintenance checks, and not driving it too fast. Respect behavior is the same way. It takes a lot of continuing attention and maintenance of the heart to produce truly respectful responses. But the effort is well worth it: It's really healthy for you and the big bonus is that the bulk of your child's respect training will take place through the soaking-up process.

Try not to be discouraged if you feel you don't "measure up" to the examples I'm going to share; I'm just trying to make the points crystal clear.

Respect is about the inside and outside of a person—the heart and the head. Thoughts and feelings come from the inside, or the heart. Comments and behaviors are expressed on the outside, or the head. Here are four guidelines to building respect that you'll see played out in the rest of this chapter. Use these guidelines for your regular maintenance checkups.

1. In some way, support the other person's inside thoughts and feelings (heart), even if you don't agree with his or her outside behavior. *Then* deal with the person's outside behavior (head). I call it the H2 approach. And sometimes a zipped mouth is the only way to go. Heart first, head second.

2. Use genuine, courteous, nonjudgmental, nonlabeling comments when problem-solving with others, especially your child. Strive for "I" statements as you describe a situation. Instead of "You always . . ." say, "When you talk mean to me, I feel hurt and put down. That's not acceptable."

3. Set firm, consistent limits when problem solving, but without a lot of fear (discomfort). Remember some stress is necessary for change. Not, "You always disappoint me (very scary for children) but "It's really hard for you to stop your blowups. Let's find some ways to make it easier to show your anger appropriately." Learning self-control and respect for authority will not happen without establishing firm limits.

4. Practice self-respect through balancing work with play. Maintain friendships, special interests, good health habits, and basic self-acceptance.

See how this plays out with the Dumont family.

So far Dad hasn't been talking much at the dinner table, and fifteen-year-old Kristen notices with this gentle comment: "Dad, you're not saying much. Are you okay?

Dad puts his fork down and does a little Morse code finger tap on the table as he gathers his thoughts. "Yeah, Kristen, today was not a good day. My boss called me into the office to let me know my sales last month were not good enough for the company. If they don't improve this month, I'll be put on probation." He looks out the window, fighting his emotions, wondering how far to go with this conversation. *I definitely don't want to tear up. But I learned in our parenting class that it's really important to show my feelings.*

Mom reaches over, gently touches his arm (Kristen's feeling really sad and a little scared), and breaks the silence. "Don, that must really be hard for you."

Dad and Mom do a quick mutual hand squeeze and he decides to share more. "It is, but my boss was concerned, as usual, about how I was taking it and let me know how much the company likes my team leadership, my optimistic attitude, and the way my work is always on time. He told me the numbers I need to produce and gave me a name of a colleague who is ready to assist me. I really appreciated him being up front about what I need to do. He even gave me tomorrow off to think things over."

Tears glisten on Kristen's cheeks as she says, "If you lose your job, will we need to move?"

Dad reaches over to put a soothing hand on Kristen's shoulder. "Kristen, I do have a job for a least three months, just in case I am put on a ninety-day probation. For now, try not to worry a lot about it. I know you're sad and scared."

Mom adds, "Kristen, one thing about your daddy. When he knows what he needs to do, he really gets at it." She shifts her eyes to look at her husband, squeezes his hand again (Kristen's watching like a hawk), and says, "I know you're worried now, but we'll work this through together. Hey, how about if I make your favorite dinner—lasagna, salad, and garlic bread—tomorrow night? And maybe you need to go more regularly to your monthly remote-control-airplane club."

Don's face brightens as a glimmer of his usual enthusiasm returns to his voice. "You're right. I think tomorrow I'll put the final touches on my model Beechcraft and get it ready for the Friday night meeting." He looks at Kristen and says, "It's really easy for me to work too much. I need to be more like you; you always have time to enjoy your friends and do fun things."

Kristen is relieved as she reflects, *I'm not so worried now. Things are so much better with Mom and Dad now. Before they went to that marriage workshop last summer, this type of deal would have ended up with Dad saying nothing, or if he did there'd be a lot of yelling between the two of them. And I always wondered when the big "D" word would come out. Now Dad talks a lot more about his feelings, and when a fight does happen Dad and Mom always make up sooner or later—right in front of me. Now when they fight, I take a deep breath and don't think much of it.*

Can you hear the respect guidelines? Kristen, Mom, and even Don's boss were speaking to Don's heart by recognizing and supporting Don's deepest feelings and needs. The first of the respect guidelines were working: Don felt supported, especially with all of Mom's positive feedback. And then Don's boss applied the respect guidelines to Don's work behavior: Firm limits were set with just the right amount of fear—the probation. (Nobody wants probation on the job.) Don's self-respect needs tweaking, but at least he's got it on his radar by planning to spend more time on his plane hobby.

Hey, Kids!

Kids, how often do you see Mom and Dad solve their problems so you know everything will be okay? Most of the time parents forget to show the solving part, and that can make kids feel uneasy. Respectfully ask your parents to let you know if they've solved their problems when you see them fight. (Parents, studies confirm that when parents show kids that their conflicts have been solved or are being worked on, self-assurance thrives, resulting in better academic and behavior performance.)

And did you know it's really healthy for you to share your emotions like Kristen did? At first sharing feelings seems kind of weird because you know most kids will laugh if you tell them your feelings. I've noticed this too. It's because most kids hardly ever use feeling words. Anyway, try it at home and ask your mom and dad if they will encourage all of your family to use feeling words. Most parents will agree to do this.

Okay, parents, I know that many of you already are doing a lot of what we just covered. Try to keep showing these things *daily* to your child. And if you can't remember the four respect guidelines, remember H2: *heart first, head second*. When you do this you are showing respect to your child and implementing the most basic Golden Rule requirement: *Start where I am.*

Now let's take a look at what's involved in establishing self-respect within your child.

Learning to Respect Myself

Nine-year-old Maggie's scowl accentuates her high-pitched answer to Mom's question: "Liam pinched me and that's why I hit him."

Mom sees Maggie make a face at Liam and responds, "I saw you—"

Maggie interrupts, repeatedly pointing her finger at Liam and then at Mom. "You're always on his side! I hate him! You don't care about me."

You know where this is headed. Maggie is sent to her room, pushing and kicking everything in sight. And Mom's thinking, *When will*

Maggie stop attacking her little brother? I can't believe she's getting so defiant.

No respect for Mom, and Maggie's self-respect is really low. Let's find out the "whys" with a quick psych eval of Maggie's situation.

Respect gets established using the Golden Rule's principle that everyone wants to be treated with respect.

When the parent respects the child, then the child's self-respect is established and the child respects others.

A child's self-respect is at the center of the whole picture. How does this apply to Maggie? Maggie's self-respect is at just one or two bars. Weak signal. And her ongoing anger and defiance are outward signs caused by her inside (heart) belief that Mom doesn't care about me. Maggie's heart translation: *I'm not lovable* (respected) *since Mom and Dad don't care for me.* (Stay with me; we're reading Maggie's emotional EKG, not what you know to be true on the outside.) When children are caught in this "don't care" trap, they may become defiant or keep their feelings inside, depending on their personality. Both are natural and unhealthy responses that make things worse for everyone, and the self-respect reading may go down to one bar or even lower.

Are you bothered with the requirement that parents must show children respect before a child's self-respect can be established? You know the old saying, "To get respect, you must give respect." Even though this saying makes a lot of sense, most parents tell me, "I'm the adult, and kids need to learn respect for authority whether I earn it or not."

I wholeheartedly agree with this "respect authority" expectation if from past experience your child can count on your validating (respecting) his or her thoughts and feelings most of the time. Establish this step in your regular parenting routine most of the time, and your child will respect your authority most of the time.

In my clinical experience, this "heart first, head second" approach is the most direct route to establishing your child's self-respect, resulting in greater respect for others.

And, yes, you know as well as I do, there are many respectful adults who have four-bar self-respect who had little to no heart–to–heart communication with their parents. But from my experience, minimal communication is high risk and results in far more failures than successes.

Back to Maggie. You know the fix by now: a lot of respectful, heart-to-heart communication. But doing it feels next to impossible when you hear comments like "You don't care about me," and you've spent your whole life working back-to-back double shifts making sure you cared—a lot. You *know* it's flat-out not true. And what makes things worse is that the reasons for Maggie's "don't care" comments are not visible; you need an emotional EKG heart reader. Maggie's reading: *I'm feeling uncared for* (unlovable); *Mom only cares for Liam.* And Maggie acts like it's set in concrete.

Let's take a quick peek at the following video clip to see what Mom does with this information from a Golden Rule perspective.

Mom's instituted a regular out-of-the house time with Maggie. Before going to the park for a picnic lunch, she reviewed her heart-to-heart cheat sheet: (1) Listen, and if you talk, ask questions; (2) receive your child's comments as heart talk—it's Maggie's inside truth for now; and (3) validate feelings, delay corrections.

Now for the clip.

"You told me you don't feel I care for you. That's pretty sad. What do you mean?"

Maggie responds. "You never send Liam to his room."

Possibly, but if Maggie would be nicer I wouldn't need to send her to her room so often. Talk to her heart (feelings). "You're right. That does happen a lot." [Remember, Mom's addressing only what Maggie sees—her head info.] "No wonder you're feeling so upset and sad [heart info]. Tell me more." *I did it! I didn't give her my worn-out "If you weren't so mean to Liam" answer.*

Now Mom's ready for two fix-it steps: (1) increased positive attention and (2) firm limit setting. (Don't get discouraged. This heart cultivating will take some weeks to pull the defiant weeds out while stimulating the growth of self-respect, which will lead to respect for others. Watch carefully and you'll see the growth happening.)

Here are two "increased attention" solutions Mom implemented: (1) daily or every other day, one-to-one attention (ten to fifteen minutes of time together—can include TV shows), bringing up things related to her dance passion (news items, TV shows); and (2) weekend time away from the house together (one to two hours).

Mom mixed in limit setting with her increased attention. She used the Discussion Procedure (chapter 6) to come up with two solutions.

First solution: Maggie will tell Mom if she feels picked on by Liam instead of hitting him. If hitting happens, Maggie would need to go to her room, write in her "feelings journal," and go over what she wrote with her mom. (Writing about feelings and new ways to handle them strengthens growth.)

Second solution: When Maggie feels uncared for or that "Liam gets all the breaks," Maggie will tell Mom.

After several weeks of practice, here's the result. Maggie reported, "Now I feel Mom's really interested in me and finally sees why I've been so upset with Liam. I guess he's not such a bad kid after all."

Throughout the process, Mom was surprised how often and how hard it was for her to edit herself and then go into "validate" mode when Maggie complained to her about Liam. However, Mom saw almost from the start that spending more time understanding Maggie made her daughter feel more respected, and self-respect was taking root in her daughter. The defiance was steadily decreasing, and there were glimmers of positive stuff happening between Maggie and Liam.

The Golden Rule formula worked: Maggie felt a lot of respect from Mom, and in turn Maggie's self-respect grew as well as her respect for Mom *and* Liam.

What does healthy self-respect in your child begin to look like? Consider these three new behaviors as evidence of progress:

1. *Seeing mistakes as opportunities for improvement.* Ten-year-old Michael makes a mistake and says, "This is a chance to make things better; I want to try." Seeing mistakes in this way means self-improvement will become a habit and will develop a strong belief that *I'm okay*. It sure is a better way of living than what Michael used to say: "I can't believe I'm so stupid." Not a good cultivation program.

2. *Correcting mistakes by owning "my part first."* Madison has just been confronted about her 3 A.M. cell phone usage and responds, "It's true, I did that; I messed up." That's not the way she handled mistakes at the beginning of her freshman year before counseling started. Mom was tearing her hair out because Madison was denying everything.

3. *Balancing hard work with healthy relationships.* Halfway through first grade, six-year-old Randy said to his dad, "Do I have to always do an hour of homework every night? I'd like to play with my friends if I could. I can never play until the weekend." In response, Mom and Dad establish a more balanced work and play routine: a reduced homework schedule and some additional playtime nightly, sometimes with friends. They also made sure Randy developed better work skills during his homework. We've seen in the past chapters that the habit of hard work (according to your child's personality) combined with plenty of time with friends and family is a great recipe for healthy children—physically, socially, and emotionally.

Make your child's heart strong with plenty of validation. A strong heart (self-respect) makes throwing away bad behavior a lot easier.

Respectful, Loving Behavior Toward Others

Follow these three guidelines from early on and you'll be quite satisfied with your child's respectful behavior.

1. **Establish, practice, and affirm good social graces.** From two years of age on, require your child to know when to say "Thank you," "Please," "May I?," "Excuse me," and any other social graces you feel are necessary. Consider handshake training by six years of age. And work toward eye contact as much as possible. You know how important first impressions are, and good social graces catch people's attention.

2. **Teach respect for authority—to talk or not to talk.** "I need the trash taken out right now," Mom says. Kyle's whiny response: "I'm watching TV. Why don't you do it." After some boot-camp respect training, Kyle responded with action and appropriate words to a similar request: "I'll get right to it," he said as he left the TV and met Mom's request. Make sure your child knows by six years of age when to not talk back to authority figures, and then reinforce the habit during the tween and teen years.

Sometimes giving one's opinion to people in authority is called for, but some advance respect training may be required. Mason's college chemistry teacher started their after-class meeting with a rather sharp comment: "You said you handed in the last class assignment, but I can't find it anywhere. You'll need to do it by tomorrow or get an F." Mason's thoughts raced: *I spent ten hours on it and I know exactly the time and place I handed it in. If I talk, I'll yell. I'll ask to talk when I can say it calmly.* "Uh, Mr. Yoder, may I meet with you tomorrow after class and talk more about it?"

At the next meeting, after a lot of role playing with Mom on the phone, Mason said calmly as he handed Mr. Yoder the ten-page rough draft of the assignment they had discussed the day before, "Here's my rough-draft work on the assignment. I remember hand-ing in my final draft. Would you consider allowing me to hand in another final draft on Monday?" Mr. Yoder spent a seeming eternity shuffling through the rough draft. Then he huffed, shook his head, and reluctantly said, "It's a deal."

Children need a lot of experience in when and how to respond to authority figures respectfully. In your daily family interaction, encourage your child to speak his or her mind respectfully in authority situations when the circumstances are right. Keep in mind it'll take a while to smooth out the rough edges.

3. ***Teach respect for friends and siblings.*** Here are two principles to help teens show respect for each other:

   1. Listen and respond positively to feelings *before* agreeing or disagreeing: "I can see how Jen not calling you for a week has really got you worried."

   2. When disagreeing—after feelings are validated—focus only on the person's point or behavior in a nonjudgmental way (no "you shoulds"). Use *I* messages: "I can see why you're so ticked about Nell spreading that rumor about you, but I'm wondering if there's another way to handle it than posting your thoughts on Facebook."

Children who have been treated respectfully by their parents are familiar with these basic respect behaviors; they've been respected, developed self-respect, and clearly know how good it feels. All they need is for parents to support them in treating others the same way they are being treated at home—with dignity and respect.

That's it for this chapter, but there's one other respectful behavior we need to address. In chapter 8 we'll discuss how to develop within your child the most priceless human respect quality: compassion—first establishing self-compassion and then compassion toward others.

CHAPTER 8

"Please Help Me Be Compassionate —First with Myself"

WITH TEARS IN HIS eyes, four days into the 2011 Libyan hostage crisis, the lead fifty-year-old Khadafy guard said, "Okay, let's try to get you out of here."

Hostage CNN producer Jomana Karadsheh had just finished pleading with him, saying, "I really miss my family . . . I really want to see my family. They're worried about me." She had spent four and a half days building a relationship with this guard, much of it exchanging family experiences, especially the guard's sadness about missing his five children.

That same day Jomana and the other thirty-four journalists were set free, unharmed. Most of them had already said their final goodbyes via cell phone to their families.

When asked how she pulled off the release, Jomana made this comment: "In the end, we're all human. And that's what this was about—connecting with him as a human" (Wayne Drash, CNN August 25, 2011).

What an example of the life-sustaining power of compassion: deep awareness of another person's feelings and suffering, and doing something about it even in a life-or-death situation.

How did Jomana know so much about compassion? Why is compassion so life-changing for both the giver and the receiver? What does it take to *consistently* walk the Golden Rule talk—to compassionately treat others the way you'd like to be compassionately treated?

We've actually been unbundling many of these answers since our first chapter. You've been trying your hand at three basic compassion tools: (1) understanding, (2) acceptance, and (3) respect—all three delivered by our fundamental Golden Rule guideline, *Start where I am.*

Our compassion capacity blossoms when respect for ourselves and others becomes a habit. We learned in the last chapter that respect is about nonjudgmental acknowledgment of *who I am* and *who you are.* Compassion is the action part of respect—*doing* in-depth acts of kindness related to what we've acknowledged within others or ourselves. For example, thanking a teacher for his kindness toward your child, or being extra kind to yourself when you're struggling to change an unhealthy habit.

We'll start with self-compassion in this chapter and then learn the ropes about compassion toward others in the next chapter. In the final chapter, we'll address the capstone for treating ourselves and others in the healthiest way possible: humility.

Here's what we'll look at in this chapter:

- How we are hard-wired for compassion
- The secrets of establishing self-compassion, which is the essential foundation for showing compassion to others

Wired for Compassion

Lucas and Claire—eighteen months and three years of age respectively—had finished their lunch and were just settled into their Saturday afternoon playtime with all their favorite toys around them.

Lucas's mom, Janice, smiles at her older brother and says, "John, how lucky we are that we live in the same town and can enjoy our kids together. Lucas will be able to form a really close bond with Claire."

John smiles and nods as he finds a comfy place on the floor next to the kids. "It's so great. I think—"

Claire has tripped over a toy and started to cry. Little Lucas looks toward Claire and frowns. He darts a fast look at his mom and then waves his arms in distress. Both parents reach out to comfort their kids. A few moments later, both kids settle down and resume their fun play.

With that proud-parent look, Janice comments." Did you see Lucas's concerned look just then? I read online that it's at about eighteen months that empathy starts to kick in. I've started to see that happen more and more with Lucas."

John shares his sister's excitement. "Isn't that something how young kids start to know how others feel? Yesterday when I was picking up Claire at preschool, I saw her best friend being pushed down. Claire went over, patted him on the back, and said, 'Sorry.' Her friend put his arms around Claire and stopped crying. It was the cutest thing."

I'm sure you've witnessed this type of scenario as well. Aren't little kids amazing? They're so spontaneous and responsive! Children clearly *feel* another person's physical and emotional pain by eighteen months of age, and by age three they are starting to do something about what they feel—the beginning of compassionate behavior.

John is a physician's assistant at the local pediatric clinic, so Janice asks, "What's going on that makes kids naturally notice feelings at such a young age?"

John puts on his professional face and responds. "We just had a workshop on this stuff. Scientists say we've got mirror neurons in our brains. When Lucas saw Claire's pain, his neurons kicked in and he actually felt, to some degree, the pain as if it were happening to him. And he reacted accordingly."

"Amazing! And is that what happened when Claire comforted that kid at preschool?"

"Yes, and there's something else. A hormone called oxytocin started flowing for both Claire and her friend when her compassion kicked in. The release of that hormone probably explains a lot of that warm feeling we all get when we give or receive things. We feel pleasure, and everything gets calmer inside. Our blood pressure goes down and our heart rate actually decreases. And here's the cool thing: The pleasure we feel in situations like this can be equal to other things that satisfy us, like food and drink."

Janice takes it all in, and then with that lightbulb-turned-on look observes, "All of that stuff must have been happening when we calmed our kids down just a minute ago." She pauses for a minute, reflecting on how she and John fought as kids, and then turns to John with a smile. "I'm sure glad we've shined up our mirror neurons as we've gotten older. I'd say oxytocin flows pretty often nowadays."

John reaches out for a high five and says, "Yeah, I sure made your life miserable in my teenage years. Wish I could do those years again—the right way this time." With a deep sigh, he shifts the subject: "Hey, what do you want for your birthday? It's coming up soon."

On multiple occasions, you've witnessed the amazing results of compassion's miracle. It's a limitless source of deep-seated pleasure when we plug in to it. Fully developed compassion is the most economical and beneficial health-care system in the world: It's a proven stress reducer, and it keeps the immune system working well. In just a minute we'll get to our next subject about how to plug in to compassion's energy source, self-compassion. But first a word to the kids.

Hey, Kids!

Kids, when you used to fall down, you remember how good it felt for Mom and Dad to hold you and say nice things like, "I know it hurts now, but it'll be okay pretty soon." How about when you've been teased at school and you start crying when you tell Mom about it and she's sad for you? Feels better, doesn't it, especially if a hug is included?

That's the good stuff that happens when people care and are kind. Adults call it compassion.

A lot of you are being encouraged by your parents and teachers to be kind as much as possible. You know, if you see that someone at school has been crying, it's great if you show you care by asking kindly if the person needs anything. Or, when someone's teased at school, you could either tell the bully to stop or tell a teacher what's going on. Or, when you've really gotten mad and hit your sister or brother, you can go say you're sorry.

Does it feel weird to do this kindness stuff? Most kids feel weird at first. It's just easier to ignore people when they're hurting. It's kind of like homework. Who wants to do it? But when you force yourself to do it, you're happy that it's done. And if you force yourself to do it every time, it becomes a habit. The same is true with being kind and feeling happy afterward.

One other thing. Sometimes when you're kind, other kids, especially boys, might make fun of you and say stuff like "You're such a sissy." That's really hard to take, especially around your friends. Kids do this because they're uncomfortable with kindness and they deal with it by putting others down. I'll admit it's hard to handle teasing, but try to ignore it or give a one-liner like "I like kindness; why don't you try it sometime?" Then make sure you leave right way. Who wants to hear more putdowns?

Establishing Self-Compassion

Deep awareness of what's going on deep inside a person and doing something about that person's feelings and suffering—that's compassion. According to our Golden Rule guideline, children need to first have personal, inner experiences of compassion before they can know how to treat others compassionately or *treat others the way I treat myself.*

This inner experience comes in two ways: (1) parents showing their children compassion and (2) children being compassionate toward themselves. Your child's been experiencing compassion from you since you started reading this book (and probably long before that) with the most basic compassionate parenting behavior: *Start where I am.* Now let's dig into what self-compassion looks like.

Here's the most important self-compassion belief you'll learn to instill within your child by the time you've finished this chapter: *For now, I understand and accept my humanness (both the good and the bad) without shame.*

Throughout my clinical experience, I've found the single biggest life hurdle for most people is learning to effectively deal with their own "bad" behaviors without shame. And self-compassion fixes the problem better than anything I've witnessed.

I got to the nitty-gritty of how to effectively deal with this problem at a recent workshop. I asked parents to tell me what was meant by the "bad" stuff everyone struggles with every day. After a lively discussion, they all settled on this conclusion: *Bad stuff happens when our basic needs are not met in a healthy way.*

So what are our basic needs? Here's the list they came up with. Everyone needs to feel

1. pleasure, now;
2. safe and secure, minimal fear;
3. independent;
4. lovable through connectedness (all aspects of intimacy); and

5. confident through successes, growth, and making a difference.

Then I asked for a volunteer to share what it's like to suffer from
bad stuff. I was glad I had remembered the tissue boxes.

Toward the back of the room, a middle-aged man stood and
cleared his throat as he clutched the seat in front of him. "I'm Gerald, father of four beautiful kids, and I'm a recovering alcoholic. All I
remember as a kid is being afraid my dad would hit me or my mom
when he was drunk."

Gerald stopped a minute to review the needs list on the board
and then continued. "I always felt insecure, and the only pleasure I
felt was escaping a whuppin', as we called them back then. According
to my parents, I was a failure at everything and a success at nothing,
even though I made the varsity basketball team in my senior year. I
really felt disconnected. And that word *shame*—that's at the heart of
it all. When you *feel* bad about everything, you start *acting* bad all
the time."

He stopped to clear his throat again, and he accepted several tissues from his wife. Dabbing his cheek, he quietly said, "Excuse me,
but I've got to say the rest. The bad behavior started in junior high. It
was such a relief to get into Dad's booze. By high school I was drink-
ing every day. The pain was gone. That first point on your list about
pleasure? The booze was the only way I could feel pleasure."

Just before he sat down, Gerald tried to look every person in
the eye. Then he said in a cracking, pleading voice, "Please, please,
everyone, help your kids know what their needs are, help them be
comfortable with all of them, and teach them how to get those needs
met in a healthy way. That's all I want to say." He sat down, cradled
his head in his hands, and sobbed.

The deafening silence was punctuated by sniffles and the sound
of tissues being pulled out of the boxes. Everyone could feel the suffering caused by *I'm bad*; everyone was privately feeling their own

version of the *I'm bad* syndrome, and everyone felt their own sadness and ravages of shame.

Near the front of the room, a middle-aged woman stood up, turned to group, and cleared her throat. "I'm Amie, mom of two precious teenage girls." Glancing at Gerald, she said in the kindest voice, "Gerald, my heart goes out to you. And I have so much respect that you squarely faced your needs and had the guts to repair a broken heart."

Turning back to the rest of us, she said, "Until I was fourteen, not one of those six needs up on the board was met in my life.

"My dad, whom I adored beyond belief . . ." She looked down and shook her head as if to clear the sadness and continued. "He worked six days a week plus overtime, and my mom only paid attention to my schoolwork, me being a 'dance prodigy,' and how I looked. She'd always say I was pudgy, especially when I was about eleven. By twelve I was failing everything at school, and the only pleasure I felt was when I pleased my mom. I remember thinking there was something wrong with me, and I asked myself, *What can I do to feel good?*

"I fixed feeling bad by lying about homework, and I did everything possible to look like a Vegas showgirl. Guess what? A lot of older guys really 'liked' me, so I started sneaking out and became completely intimate by age fifteen. If you look at those needs up there, from where I was coming from, I was finally feeling loved, significant, pleasure, secure, and very successful.

"Anyway, I was lucky. My dad caught me with one of my midnight dates in a car, and everything changed after that. If I told you all the details, we'd be here until tomorrow morning."

Up to then, everyone in the crowd had been sitting like statues, most of them with mouths open in disbelief. Now they all chuckled, looking at each other and whispering, anxiously awaiting the rest of the story.

Amie looked to her left and said, "Dad, lay it on 'em."

A sixty-something, well-groomed man slowly stood. "I'm not going to give you all the gory details," he began, "but when I found her with that guy, a switch flipped inside me for the first time. It took about a day for me to start seeing where the problem was—me." He looked at his wife, who was dressed like a model, and she pointed to herself and whispered, "Me, too."

"So we all ended up in counseling. It started with family therapy, and we soon added marital counseling. At first it seemed like a lot of money and time, and we struggled with whether it was worth it all.

"But it was worth every penny. Our focus became family relationships and seeing people for who they really are. I guess you could say we stopped expecting others to be just like us. And the buck stopped with me. I began carving out more weekly family time and spending at least an hour of one-to-one time every week with Amie. And we had to learn patience. It took a while for our situation to get this bad, and it took a while to see improvements. Now and then we got discouraged. Seems like we took a few steps backward just when we thought we were making progress. But our therapist said not to worry; it's just part of the journey."

Amie's mom stood, smiled at her family, and added, "The more we showed acceptance and understanding, the more Amie got to know herself. Pretty soon things really started to turn around for her. Within a year Amie had stopped dance, started getting As and Bs, and become involved in art—her real passion."

Trying to make eye contact with as many people as possible, Mom observed, "The hardest thing for me was to really listen to Amie. It meant accepting everything she felt, which tended to be way different than the way I felt about things. Her anger was really hard to take at first. I still struggle with really listening." She pulled some tissues from the box and lightly dabbed under her eyes, then continued. "I can tell you things really changed big time when I started listening and accepting instead of yelling at her. Our therapist said it's common for parents to get mad and basically fall into a shame-and-blame trap. Feelings get buried, and then everything and everyone heads south." She looked down and said quietly, "Sounds horrible just hearing myself say it."

Amie stood again, put her arm around her mom's shoulder, and said to the group, "I was lucky. I got to know both sides of the human fence. On the one side, I saw the bad stuff that happens when those basic needs you wrote on the board are not dealt with in a healthy way. On the other side, I saw how much easier life is, most of the time, when I can be compassionate and nice toward myself when I'm trying to improve things."

Amie and her mom hugged and sat down; everyone broke into applause.

After several more people gave their life stories, I asked the group to tell me what they had just learned about self-compassion.

Leah nailed it. "When Amie's parents got things straight, Amie got who she really was—good and bad—reflected back to her by both parents, compassionately." She turned and looked admiringly at Amie's family. "And you guys did it with encouragement instead of 'Why can't you do it right for once?' I'm sure you don't do it all the time, but you clearly did it enough. Wow, I've got a long way to go."

Then Eric added, "Amie, you sure got a big dose of compassion up close and personal. What's making sense to me now is that parental compassion and kids being compassionate to themselves is something that almost happens together. I've never thought of it that way. Pretty cool. I guess when a parent's compassionate to a kid, it greases the child's self-compassionate gears. Hmm . . ." He sat down, smiling and nodding in agreement with himself.

Hey, Kids!

Kids, what do you think? It's kind of hard to believe, but your bad stuff doesn't have to make you feel you're a bad person. When you learn that bad thoughts and behavior happen to everybody, you don't have to beat yourself up so much. You can be kinder to yourself as you fix mess-ups, saying things like *I'll work harder to remember my chores and ask Mom and Dad to encourage me as much as possible.* I know that sounds weird but does telling yourself I'm so stupid really help at all? Your mom and dad are going to help you think and talk with a lot more compassion. Try it, I think you'll like it.

I hope you now have a good idea of how to establish self-compassion within your child. If so, the foundation is in place to train your child to be compassionate toward others. Follow the guidelines in the next chapter and I think you'll be pleased with the outcome.

CHAPTER 9

"... And Help Me Be Compassionate with Others"

Be kind and compassionate to one another,
forgiving each other, just as in Christ God
forgave you. (Ephesians 4:32)

HAVE YOU EVER HEARD of a Certified Compassion Curriculum (K–12 training program) or a CP (Compassionate Person) degree? They don't exist. Have you ever heard of an Outstanding Compassionate Person of the Year award being bestowed at a high school commencement? I haven't.

Compassion toward others is "nice," but, really, is it that important? Good grades, being better than someone else, being popular, winning, getting a degree, and being financially successful—that's what *really* brings success and happiness. Right?

No, not according to the Golden Rule approach to parenting. Success and happiness don't start and end with the "outside" aspects of life. It's all about how we would like to be treated on the inside—with respect and compassion—and then learning to treat others in the same way we were treated. Inner satisfaction with "who I am" is the starting point, the foundation for all outside happiness, and a big part of this inner satisfaction is the difference that a heart for God can make in your life and the life of your child. We don't always heed the Spirit's guidance, but when we do, genuine kindness and compassion for others will flow from within because God himself is kind and compassionate. You and your child actually become his vessels for extending God's kindness and compassion to others.

Learning and Practicing Compassion

We're just in time to witness a training session between two-and-a-half-year-old Ruby and her mom. (But be assured we'll cover all three age groups in this chapter: preschool, school age, and high school.) As we listen in to Mom and Ruby, I'll add my running commentary in parentheses.

Ruby's so excited. The world is hers to take over. She's in what experts call the *trust/autonomy* stage of child development: "Don't get in my way!" It's really hard for Mom to be compassionate when it seems "No" is every other word out of Ruby's month. As we watch Mom in action with Ruby, keep two early-childhood developmental needs in mind. Subconsciously (because she can't yet put these needs into words) little Ruby is thinking:

- "I need to establish physical and emotional trust in my parents and eventually myself."
- "I need to feel good about all the new stuff I'm doing and not feel too much doubt and shame when I mess up."

Mom asserts, "Ruby, you can't go outside; it's too cold."

Ruby starts whining and thinks, *I'm going outside and I can't stop whining.* There's little to no self-control at this age, but teaching self-control must start right away. It takes more than eighty repeats to establish a new behavior.

"I know you're upset and you should be," Mom acknowledges. (Used in this way, *should* is a compassionate word, helping Ruby learn to accept all of her feelings as part of *who I am*.) Mom continues. "If you continue to show you're upset by whining, you'll need to whine in your room, not here." (Compassionate limit setting teaches healthy self-control. It sets the stage for Ruby to start practicing her own compassionate self-control when she's correcting her mistakes.)

And there are plenty of opportunities for Ruby to learn compassion toward others. Earlier in the day, Mom had said, "Ruby, can you give your little sister her rattle? Maybe it will help her stop crying."

Simultaneously, Ruby feels two opposite ways toward her sister: *No, she's annoying and I'm busy*; and *I'm upset when I hear her cry and I want to help*. (Remember the mirror neuron connection?)

This time, Ruby hands the rattle to her sister. Little Kathryn stops crying and Ruby smiles.

So Mom says, "Ruby, that was so kind of you to stop your play to help Kathryn when she was sad. Come here so I can hug you." (Giving reasons, stating feelings words, and celebrating successes combined with physical affection help compassion's root systems get established.) Ruby smiles, runs to Mom, and gets her hugs. The oxytocin's flowing and it's likely that several more mirror-neuron connections were created in the brains of both Ruby and Kathryn. (It's true! Neurons can increase when exercised.)

Another mom, just down the street, is training four-year-old Riley, who's having a blast being with other kids—especially his preschool friend Lola. Experimenting big time with self-initiation is the four-year-old's primary developmental task. Two needs take center stage in Riley's perspective:

- "I love being in control and powerful. But when I have too much control, people get mad and I feel bad."
- "I love being with all kinds of people. If only they'd do what I want."

Mom's fixing a snack as she observes Riley and Lola having fun with their animal coloring book. And then out of nowhere, Lola starts crying while she tries to retrieve the crayon Riley had just grabbed from her.

Riley smacks her hand away and screams, "That's my crayon!"

Mom races over, takes hold of Riley's hand, gets the crayon away, and leads him to his room. "You can't hit when you're mad," she says. With his appendages flailing every which way, Riley protests, "She can't have my best crayon!"

After several minutes in his room, Mom cuddles a calmed-down Riley and gently acknowledges, "Those are your crayons and it's really hard to share. And it made you really mad when she took it. It's okay to be mad, but it's not okay to hit." (Compassionate teaching: kindly separating okay feelings from not-okay behavior). "Do you think Lola liked that crayon too? (Way to go, Mom. Compassion neurons get switched on better through kind training instead of the "you know better" type of comments most of us are inclined to use. "Shame neurons," if there are such things, lead to a dead end.)

"Yeah, but—"

Mom interrupts gently while stroking her son's back. "Shhh. She likes that crayon just like you do. Think so?"

Riley frowns, but his mirror neurons are turning on. "Yeah, Mom, she does."

"It's really hard to give up something you like so the other person can be happy, but sometimes we need to do stuff like that. And at first we get mad like you did and we feel like hitting. I'll help you to handle your upset without hitting." (Briefly repeating the reasons for a new behavior serves as a rich miracle-grow treatment for planting and establishing that new behavior. And remember I'm giving you a lot of detail to ensure clarity. Saying these things in your own way is really what's most important.)

Riley frowns again, gives Mom the cutest half-smile, and says, "I'll let her use my crayon, Mommy." He runs to the table, picks up the crayon, runs to Lola, and says kindly, "You can have the crayon. Sorry."

I can hear a lot of you thinking, *I do that a lot already.* (Keep up the good work). Or maybe you're wondering, *Who has the time to do that? Whose kid behaves like that?* Keep in mind that Riley's mom has already completed more than sixty training sessions with this new non-grabbing behavior. (Remember, it takes about eighty times to get a new behavior established.)

And Riley's a fast learner. He's one of the 40 percent of children who are "easy." Don't get discouraged if you have a more difficult child. The training procedure needs to be the same, but don't expect the results to be as smooth as we've just seen with Riley. Do expect, however, to make noticeable progress each time you implement the procedure.

Let's fast-forward to six- to eleven-year-old children. This is the stage of life where you put on the training wheels and see how your child can behave without your 25/8 supervision. It's your child's first independent experience with unlimited social and academic opportunities, and here's the fundamental developmental need:

- "It's so much fun to learn as much as I can and find as many friends as I can. But nobody told me how hard it is when things don't work out, especially without Mom and Dad around."

Let's see what compassion-learning opportunities are available for six-year-old Tyler.

Three weeks into the first grade, Tyler's riding his bus to school. He thinks as he watches the trees fly by his window, *I can't wait to see Mia; she's so fun to chase. How can she hang on the monkey bars so long?. . . Other kids get the subtraction stuff, but I don't. Guess I'll try my hardest like Mom says and—*

Two rows up a kid yells at Tyler's friend Ned, "You're such a nerd!"

Ned starts crying and the bus driver yells over his shoulder, "Knock it off, Jake, or I'll give you a pink slip."

Tyler tenses up and thinks, *That's so mean . . . I can't cry . . . stop . . . What if Jake teases me?*

As Tyler gets off the bus he wants to comfort Ned but isn't sure what to do. That night as Dad tucks him in bed, Tyler is extra quiet. Dad asks with a gentle stroke of Tyler's hair, "Something bothering you?"

Tyler whispers, "I was scared today when a kid teased Ned. I was sad for Ned. What should I do?" (If this sounds too perfect, it's not. Six-year-old children who have learned "heart talk" can express feelings really well even if they are difficult children.)

Dad pecks Tyler on the cheek. "That's so kind of you to feel sad for Ned. What would you like to do?"

"Could I put my hand on his shoulder like you guys do to me and say, 'I'm sad about what that kid did to you?'"

Dad smiles, signals a high five, and the big hand and little hand make a perfect smack. Dad says, "That's exactly right. Before you go to school tomorrow we'll practice. You know how we've practiced before with this sort of thing." (Learning a new behavior is turbo-charged with practice. Role playing with your child helps a lot.)

"Yeah, Dad, that'd be fun."

"We'll talk tomorrow about how to deal with that guy who teased Ned. Just so you know, kids who tease other kids are sometimes pretty unhappy themselves, and they handle it by being mean. Maybe he doesn't have friends or he feels stupid at school. It's important to stop mean behavior but also to understand what's in the kid's heart—you know, what's hurting him—and then find a way to be nice. We'll talk more about it tomorrow." (Remember, making sense of a problem helps a lot, especially when there's compassionate understanding of another person's negative behavior.)

Tyler snuggles closer to Dad, looks into his eyes, and says, "Yeah, Dad, Ned always gets the wrong answers in math. He even cried the other day when he got a zero."

Dad tells a brief bedtime story, Tyler's breathing gets slower and deeper, and dreamland takes over. Dad turns out the light and, full of wonder, takes one last look at Tyler—such a precious human being lying peacefully in bed. Dad's eyes moisten as he thinks, *It's so satisfying to hear how caring and aware Tyler is about people.* (And thank you, Dad, for your compassionate style. We can see you've been doing this for a while now.)

Hey, Kids!

Kids, you face this stuff every day—problems with other kids or your friends or how hard it is to learn things at school. Some days are great, and other days you just don't feel like going to school. I've got an answer to make it better, and you've heard it from me before: Pay attention to all of your feelings, good and bad—both are important—and share them with your parents. Ask them what to do. Your parents really want to know and help, or they wouldn't be reading this book.

Parents, I'm sure you've been through situations similar to those we've covered here. Compassion-learning opportunities are everywhere every day. Mine these teachable moments every chance you get, and keep in mind four compassion-building guidelines that we've witnessed with Tyler and Ruby:

- Encourage and validate the expression of *all* feelings, especially the difficult ones: anger, sadness, and fear. Don't forget to disconnect outside behavior from inside heart feelings (remember H2). Do set firm limits on misbehavior to encourage healthy self-control. Fully developed compassion (including humility) requires healthy self-control.

- Find *daily* opportunities to teach, experience, and practice compassion. Use the endless events found in newspapers, Internet, TV stories, grocery store situations, school experiences, or driving scenarios.

- Give brief reasons for the compassion behavior and thoughts you are teaching. It's the glue that makes the new behavior stick.

- Celebrate compassion successes and normalize failures. Make mistakes a no-shame zone.

Now for tween Terry. She's kicked off the training wheels and is entering her teen years. Terry's making every possible effort to become completely independent and to be successful *every time*. And Katy-bar-the-door if she stumbles. These are the years in which competency beliefs are being established: "I want to be sure I can do things. Will I ever feel that way?" Successes need to be the predominant experience. Some successes need to come from Terry independently learning from her mistakes—without shame. (Too many failures will breed toxic inferiority.)

Let's see how compassion-building experiences can build competency for Terry.

Once a month, Terry's family has a tradition of helping an elderly couple, the Edmonds. This month is different, however. Terry scowls at her mom and says, "I don't want to help those stupid old people clean up their yard. They can get someone else to do it. I want to hang out with my friends."

Terry's also begun fighting Friday night family time. "It's boring. Can't I just be excused so I can catch up with my Facebook friends?"

Disturbing? Yes, because you don't want to raise a selfish, self-absorbed child. And no, because self-centeredness is normal and a *necessary* "getting to know me" *beginning* part of the super-independent tween and teen years. Consider this challenging time the basis for healthy transformation into becoming a self-assured, others-compassionate young adult.

Don't close the book—I know it sounds crazy to support self-centeredness, but stay with me. I'll be the first to admit that staying calm in these situations is like swimming upstream against a strong current.

Consider first a typical answer to Terry's refusal to help the elderly couple.

Mom's voice matches her strained look. "Terry, you know the Edmonds are in their late eighties and they're really sick . . ." After several more choice lecture points Mom says, "You've got everything; it's really important to . . ." You know the rest. Of course, Terry's interrupting and rolling her eyes throughout Mom's monologue.

Remember how we said respect develops over time within a growing child? The same holds true for compassion:

Parent-to-child compassion grows a child's self-compassion, which develops a child's compassion to others.

With that formula in mind, here's the Golden Rule answer: (*Parent-to-child compassion*): "Terry, it's really hard to do something for others when you want to do your own thing. Tell me more."

(*Child's self-compassion—at the starting point of development*): "Yeah, Mom. I just want to spend Saturday afternoon with Anna. We have so much fun together." (I know this is self-centered on Terry's part, but we need to validate her starting point for the moment and work our way toward other compassion.)

Mom responds: "Anna's such a great friend. I'm so proud of how you've picked such a good friend." They talk more about what's so fun about the relationship. (I know it takes more time—a whole five minutes—to do this validation phase. And when the steam is really built up, it takes a lot of energy to keep the lid on. But as we've seen over and over, if your child feels at least somewhat validated for the way she feels, your important *future* points have a much better chance to make sense and stick.)

Mom says, "I got it. Being with Anna is a heck of a lot more fun than being with the Edmonds. But it's really important to feel for others who are suffering or need help and find time to do something for them. I know, stuff like this isn't any fun *at first*, but it can be more satisfying when we force ourselves to experience helping others. Let's not discuss it any more. You don't have a choice on this one."

Hey, Kids!

Kids, don't you hate it when your parents put their foot down? But when you think about it, what you want right away sometimes isn't the best choice. At first it's not easy to do things for others, but try not to pout too long and try to get into giving to others sometimes. It really can end up being pleasurable once you get into the habit of it. Hang in there—parents do usually know what's best.

Parents, this tween period is when you start to put the compassion-building pedal to the metal. As you saw Mom do with Terry, always start by validating your teen's normal self-centeredness and gradually work in compassion toward others.

Help needy people together once a month and take advantage of the numerous teachable moments that occur within a normal week. Demonstrate compassion in your own life and then encourage your child to see and understand the suffering of other people, whether in the neighborhood, at church, or at school. Encourage turning this understanding into acts of kindness at least once a week.

Now for the teen years. Remember how the overriding need in your three-year-old sounded like this: "Me do it"? Well, your teenager says pretty much the same thing; his language skills are just a bit better developed: "I'm finding out for myself who I am. Don't get in my way. I know what I'm doing—kind of."

So fasten your seatbelts. Let's see what part compassion can play in these exciting times.

The teen stage of life is a transformation period from Mom and Dad's way to the teen's way in an all-out effort to meet the five basic human needs: pleasure, security, independence, love, and *confidence* (chapter 7). Compassion is the central ingredient for healthy transformation, and all of us want three healthy transformations for our teens:

- Transforming from self-centeredness to compassionate self-assuredness: "Developing confidence in my strengths and comfort transforming failure into success."

- Transforming self-assuredness into humility: "I'm no better and no worse than anybody else. We've all got good and bad things about us, and everyone makes a lot of mistakes. Being kind and understanding with myself and others is the only way."

- Transforming humble self-assuredness into daily compassion toward others: "Because I know and accept my heart, I can now see into the heart of someone else because everyone's heart is basically the same. I want to celebrate their good and care for what's not so good just like my parents did for me. It's really pleasurable when it becomes a habit."

Here it is from the Golden Rule perspective: "When I feel understood, I learn to accept my humanness, especially the different and not-so-good stuff about me. That sure beats shame. Everyone else has feelings just like I have feelings, so I want to get good at understanding others like I was understood. Seems like that's what life's all about—everyone dealing with life's ups and downs together."

Let's spend the last few pages of this chapter with two transformed teens.

Strengthening the Right Things

I can always count on Mom and Dad to notice when I do something right (lovable, building confidence). *And I notice they seem to get more excited about how I like to care for others more than how much I scored in a basketball game. It's funny how the after-school tutoring I do once a week really does feel good* (pleasure, loving). *Seems like that experience keeps coming up in my head more than me getting*

MVP last month (loving, healthy human connection; compassion becoming a habit).

The other day I noticed something kind of weird. There's nothing in the graduation program next week about awarding kids for caring about others. All I saw was the valedictorian award and how many kids got full-ride academic or sports scholarships. I wonder why.

And to underscore the point, here's the opposite heart talk that happens when transformation goes south (which happens far too often): *Every time I come home I can count on doing something wrong* (no confidence or felt love). *I've got to shut this junk off. That marijuana I tried yesterday sure felt good* (destructive pleasure). *I didn't have to think about stuff anymore* (no self-compassion or other-compassion, just self-absorption; basic needs are being met destructively).

Compassion Toward Others Feels Good

Here's a typical story I hear from teens who have had good compassion training.

My folks always made a big deal about taking time for others. I remember when I was six that they sponsored an orphan in Africa. It was so cool to see the pictures of Gabrielle smiling when she received the doll we got her. I couldn't stop grinning (love through human connection). *Her pictures were so fun to see on the fridge.*

And then there was that bully in the third grade, putting down everyone and hitting kids. Mom went to the teacher about it, and they also taught me what they called "stand up for yourself skills with compassion." You know the type where you make yourself look confident: Stand straight and do a one-liner that's not hurtful: "I wish you could find a way to feel better about yourself than to put me down." Before I learned this stuff, I just wanted to run away; and if I was tougher I really would have liked to have hit that kid. That was hard to be understanding when I felt so hurt, but it really worked because I felt I was in control in a decent way (confident, successful!).

Oh, the really big thing was last summer's yearly mission trip, this time to Costa Rica. Kind of a downer at first because I missed soccer camp. But seeing the eyes of those little kids who went to the school we helped build—I've never felt anything like that before. I'm going back for the whole summer next year.

Does this sound like dreamland? Or maybe you're thinking, My kid isn't even close to that; I'm such a failure. Please don't feel that way. Compassion training isn't natural; it certainly isn't the emphasis of our typical parenting "consequence" programs or our schools' "3 Rs" curriculum. These are stories about compassion *possibilities*— possibilities that *really can come true* if we regularly plug in to our child's compassion wiring. The inside and outside warmth and satisfaction of compassion's radiant light makes all the effort worthwhile.

Speaking of radiant light, do you have one of those lightbulbs that has three levels of brightness? Well, in the next chapter we're going to find out how to switch compassion's brightness to an even greater level in your child—through humility.

CHAPTER 10

"Please Help Me Learn Humility"

Finally, all of you, live in harmony with one another; be sympathetic, love as brothers, be compassionate and humble. (1 Peter 3:8)

HAVE YOU HEARD ABOUT the new uPhone being developed by the Humble Pie (HP) Company? Saying "You" instead of "I" is required in 95 percent of conversations. And "I" is only allowed when the "Non-bragging" button is turned on. Two other buttons flash based on the receiver's needs: the SWIA (Start Where I Am) button and the RCA (Respect and Compassion with Assurance) button. And, the company is developing wireless technology to connect heart-feeling signals to the uPhone.

Okay, so I'm a dreamer. Nobody's invented a uPhone. But it sure would be nice if there were an easy way to teach humility. It's a such a life-sustaining character trait for all of us to achieve, and it's especially needed for your child. Everyone likes to feel noticed and valued. That's humility's job—*showing selfless interest in others most of the time*. The result: boundless joy for everyone. Helping your child develop genuine humility is the subject of this chapter.

The Bible is big on humility, Proverbs 18:12 says, "Before his downfall a man's heart is proud, but humility comes before honor." In other words, while society and peers tend to value a prideful, full-of-myself spirit, the Bible says that true honor and happiness come from a spirit of humility—of putting the interests of others first. Great advice for adults and children alike. Imagine what our world would be like if everyone practiced true humility! Not going to happen this side of heaven, but you can't go wrong making your part of the world a better place by teaching your child the joy and fruit of humility. It's not only sound advice, but it's the absolute Truth from our Creator himself.

It's been quite a journey getting here, but the prep work's done. Our Golden Rule parenting approach of *treat others as you would like to be treated* has served as a handy GPS, giving us step-by-step directions for treating your child the way you would like to be treated. In a lot of ways, it's been about shoes—stepping out of our comfy slippers and respectfully, compassionately, and with assurance (RCA), fitting into our child's often uncomfortable shoes (SWIA).

As we've seen in a child's early years, it's really uncomfortable to fully feel a two-year-old child's overpowering need to have it "my way." And what about feeling along with your drama queen's high-level intensity-of-reaction personality trait when you're an easy-going mom? Well, that's quite a feat. If only Dr. Scholl had developed super-cushiony parenting insoles.

Speaking of insoles, the Golden Rule journey has revealed your child also has an in-"soul," the heart, where all communication needs to start. We learned some important information about the heart: The voice of the heart is feelings; every child wants to be good; and from the get-go children are eagerly seeking to meet their five basic needs: *pleasure, security, independence, love,* and *confidence.* We've found how tricky it can be to develop your child's heart so he or she treats others the way all individuals want to be treated.

The good news is that when we establish respect and compassion for self and others we take most of the trickiness out of the situation, especially when communication starts with feelings. And you may not have known it, but you've been teaching humility along the way with SWIA; you've been selfless in your attention toward your child. And here's the touching response I hear regularly from children who have parents like you: "My mom and dad really care for me." I'm sure your child feels the same way.

When your child feels this care from you, all kinds of great things happen. Ten-year-old Patrick knows the joy of being loved just the way he is—red hair, freckles, funny, and really active. Teen Andrea feels secure and confident because she's living her dream of being a dancer. We've witnessed how children can learn to feel connected, significant, and self-assured—eventually in a healthy, non-conceited way. Those are the results of humble parenting, putting your own expectations aside and respectfully understanding and accepting your child's individuality. The essential parenting task of setting firm limits to establish good behavior, thoughts, and beliefs is most effective when this critical foundation is in place.

So, congratulations! You've been planting the seeds of humility and I'm sure you already can see some "sprouts" showing up. Now it's time to get back into your comfy slippers, settle in to that recliner, and breathe a well-deserved sigh or two. In this chapter I want to share three ground rules I've found helpful as you develop your child's humility capacity.

1. Stay on level ground; keep short tethers attached.
2. Make failures mine and successes yours—(the great life leveler).
3. Make others "home."

1. Stay on Level Ground; Keep Short Tethers Attached

Let's get the dictionary work out of the way first. The word *humble* is derived from the Latin word *humus*, meaning earth or ground. So our approach needs to be well grounded. The Greek word for humble is *praus*—"strength under control." We've learned that fully meeting our five basic needs—pleasure, independence, security, love, and confidence—establishes strength. This strength is required to control our human tendencies so our self-centered orientation can be transformed into selfless interest toward others most of the time.

So let's start with the first down-to-earth humility rule: *Stay on level ground; keep short tethers attached.*

There's no doubt about it. Flying high is so exhilarating—but too much of it keeps humility out of reach.

Everyone could see that five-year-old Brianna had a gift for piano playing. She was already playing in concerts when she was eight. Two hours of practice six days a week was paying off. By middle school her after-school hours were filled up with piano practice and homework.

So what's this got to do with staying on level ground, our first humility rule? Her parents were giving up a lot of their lives for Brianna to develop her passion. Check off humble parenting; that's selfless for sure. But Brianna was feeling increasingly stressed and she rarely spent time with friends. Family time was nonexistent. Herein lies the problem: A healthy humble person must continually be grounded by the meeting of his or her five basic needs listed above. None of these needs were being met adequately for Brianna, resulting in too much stress—not good for the heart or the head.

What's the humility-building lesson? *Performance-oriented living significantly increases the risk of establishing a self-oriented adult.* The emphasis on performance as a way to feel pleasure, independence, confidence, security, and love (or lovableness) does not adequately ground a person for establishing humility—or health for that matter.

As we've learned throughout this book, the Golden Rule approach fosters a well-grounded life by first fulfilling the child's basic needs—making sure there's plenty of respect and compassion toward oneself and others—and then making the best effort possible to achieve good things in relationships, work, and play. Humility skills thrive when this rock-solid Golden-Rule foundation is in place.

Here's the sweet and simple humility guideline: Stay grounded by meeting basic human needs, both yours and your child's; help your child stay attached to a short tether to keep from flying too far away from the Golden-Rule basics.

Here are two skills that have helped parents keep their children on level ground: Treat everyone as a diamond in the rough, and enjoy a teeter-totter life—you and me.

Treat Everyone as a Diamond in the Rough

Amanda's temper tantrums are really getting old. As Mom drags two-year-old Amanda to her room for the eighty-first time (Okay, so it might take more than eighty times to change a behavior) she thinks, *Where are those earplugs? This has got to be what "terrible" meant in that parenting book I read last week. Thank goodness her two-year checkup is this afternoon.*

Fast forward to the doctor's office later that day. Mom reviewed the tantrum play-by-play, and the doctor smiled and said, "Amanda's predominant personality trait is intensity of reaction, and when you mix in the wonderful twos, well, tantrums are often the norm. Amanda's willfulness is really a diamond in the rough. Her stubbornness will eventually serve her well. Let's discuss some ways to smooth out the rough edges."

Mom left the office revitalized with some new ideas.

Believe it or not, Amanda is experiencing humility from her mom—the same thing your child receives from you: selfless involvement even when there's often a lot of frustration. And deep down, Amanda's experiencing the gift of humility: *Even though I'm really causing a lot of trouble, Mom's still spending a lot of time caring for me when she could be doing other things.*

In my counseling practice, that is the type of comment I eventually hear from every child by seven or eight years of age. I always ask two questions as teaching points (and I suggest you try it, too): (1) "How does this 'caring' feel?" and (2) "How could you be more caring with your annoying sister?" We then discuss ways to care, and that's the assignment between sessions.

Always help your child expand "feeling words" like *caring* or *anger* into more words and thoughts. For example, *caring*: "You holding me when I'm upset really feels good"; *anger*: "I'm glad I learned to say 'I'm angry' instead of whining." The more your child knows and feels the heart language of feelings, the more humility will take root. Humility's lifeblood is knowing and successfully dealing with feelings.

Hey, Kids!

Kids, is this "diamond in the rough" idea making any sense? It does sound strange, doesn't it? Well, here's the deal. Maybe you already know it, but diamonds are super valuable and make pretty much everybody really happy (ask Mom). But they're rough looking when they're first dug out of the ground. After all, they started forming eighty miles below the surface of the earth, so they need a lot of polishing before they can sparkle.

We're all a bit like newly dug-up diamonds. We can be pretty rough sometimes when we say mean things or blow up when we don't get our way. Down deep inside, almost everyone wants to be nice, but we need a lot of human polishing—like when parents understand our mess-ups and help us be better people. Then, before long the nice parts start to show up a lot more often. Our lives sparkle more and more just like a diamond.

You need to do the same thing with your friends and even kids you don't know very well by mentioning good things about them. You can say something like "You're really a great soccer player." It's *really* hard to do this with a bully. Say a kid calls you "stupid." That's the rough diamond stuff. First say something back—a firm (not mean) one-liner: "Sounds like saying mean things is really important to you." Then confidently turn around and leave. I know you're thinking, *Who could think that fast and be that sure?*

You can, when you get really sure of yourself—when you work hard to be self-respectful and self-compassionate like we talked about in the last two chapters. Then you can be respectful and compassionate toward others, helping them and noticing what's good about them. Even bullies. And when you notice other people more and puff yourself up less, that's what adults mean by being humble.

Here are two things you can do with a problem kid: (1) Think kind thoughts (for example, *This guy must really be an unhappy person who doesn't know how to do nice things*) and (2) Do something nice (for example, say hi to him nicely when you see him in the hallway). Get your mom or dad to help you practice at home treating a mean person kindly instead of being mean back. You'll get a special good feeling once you get the hang of it.

Enjoy a Teeter-totter Life—You and Me

For the past three months, seventeen-year-old David's been receiving weekly counseling for his depression, and he's within several sessions of successful termination. He started this session with a smile as he said, "You're not going to believe who I talked to. Come on, I know you can read minds. Guess?"

"Um, let's see. . . ." I tilt my head and squint at him. "It wouldn't be Samantha, would it?" (Samantha was his year-long girlfriend who dumped him four months ago, the girl he was planning to live with after high school graduation.)

David's smile lights up the room. He gets up and goes to the whiteboard where I have a teeter-totter drawing labeled *The Humility Teeter-totter Life*. He reads out loud the three words underneath it: *uplifting, balancing, iTime*.

"You know how we've been talking about handling my breakup with Samantha with humility? Well, I think it finally sank in. I decided it was time to stop my pity party and care about Sammie's feelings. Isn't that what we've been talking about in our last couple of sessions?"

I lean forward and ask, "What happened?"

"This teeter-totter thing's really making sense." Pointing to one teeter-totter seat and then to the other, he says, "While we were dating, she was on one side and I was on the other; always a lot of ups and downs, especially toward the end. I'd uplift her by moving my end of the teeter-totter to the ground; you know, noticing her good stuff. She'd do the same thing for me. A lot of times we'd just both stay in midair, kind of a "balanced" relationship, so to speak.

He pauses and studies the *iTime* word, then turns to me and says, "It just hit me. I hardly ever did the *iTime* part, taking time for myself. That would have made me a lot stronger, you know, *strength under control*. Anyway, this week I got back on the teeter-totter with Sammie and did the lifting-her-up part. Do you wanna hear what happened?"

I can't believe my ears. David had done a lot of work to heal his hurt, especially accepting the part he played in the breakup. I move to the edge of my chair and say, "Are bluebirds blue? Yes, go on."

"I asked her out to Starbucks and told her how much I appreciated all the stuff that was great about her, how I had benefited from the relationship, and that I wanted us to be friendly with each other.

She was really happy and said she'd like to be friendly, too."

The rest of the session was spent making sure this kiln-fired lesson was deposited deeply into David's humility memory bank.

I'm sure many of you have been involved in similar acts of humility throughout your life. Tell your children about these experiences, even the times when you weren't so humble. True-life humility examples are powerful teaching lessons, especially from parents.

One of the most dramatic examples of humility I've heard involved Victoria Lindsay. On March 30, 2008, Victoria was brutally beaten by six female gang members. At the trial, she asked the judge to minimize punishment. One girl got fifteen days' jail time plus probation, and the others got off with probation only—and they had been up on felony charges. Victoria's message was loud and clear to me: "My pain is not as important as your gain." I really don't know if I could have done what she did. What an inspiration.

Now we're ready for the next ground rule that will help us to humbly cope with failures and successes.

2. Make Failures "Mine" and Successes "Yours" (the Great Life Leveler)

I'd like to invite you to watch an RCA (Respect, Compassion with Assurance) group session. Don't worry, we've got a one-way mirror set up so the teens will not be bothered. This is our second session on humility and the fifth overall session.

All five teens scurry into the room to find their seats. Nan barely gets settled and raises her hand. "Hey, Mr. Unruh, I did the SWOPI (Start Where the Other Person Is.)"

The kids love the funny sound of SWOPI ("swoh-pie").

"Yeah, my mom said it's pretty cool for an eighth grader to be understanding of a big sister who gets—"

"Tell us what you did that was so great," interrupts Brandy.

"Well, you know how we talked about blaming others right away when there's a problem. And Mr. Unruh helped us see how usually we're doing something wrong, too." Turning to Leon, Nan says, "Remember last session, Leon, when you finally admitted that your mom yells because you don't do things right away and you always argue? And by the way, did you go home and admit that stuff like you promised?"

Leon takes a big breath, blows the air out slowly, surveys most of the kids for how they're reacting, and admits, "Yeah, but I waited until two nights ago." He looks at me with a fake angry look and continues. "Next time, let kids know how hard it is to feel sure enough about yourself to pull this stuff off." He points to the whiteboard where *RCA* is written in red. "It took me a while to feel the "A" part up there—enough assurance within myself to plead guilty."

He looks back at Brandy. "Yep, I said it, and it's crazy what happened. Mom started crying and hugging me. Yuck. Then that night I just did what she asked—it was really hard to put my stuff aside—and she started bawling again."

Levi redirected the conversation back to Brandy. "Brandy, tell us what you did."

Brandy responded. "Well, you know how I said my sister is always dissing me and all of you asked what I part I was doing? I said it could be that I was always correcting her on stuff she says. The role-playing we did in here last time about how to tell my sister really helped.

"Well, I apologized to my sister and said I can see why correcting her would make her so mad." She looks at Leon. "And, Leon, I'm like you. I couldn't get up the nerve until last night to tell her. Guess what she did? She dissed me again."

She looks at me and complains, a little tongue-in-cheek, "I thought she'd be happy. Anyway, Mom heard her, put on that prison-warden look, and sent her to her room. They had a powwow in there and then my sister comes out—Mom right next to her—and apologizes to me. Then she says she appreciates me admitting what really makes her mad. It was kinda fake, like a speech. She's been nicer, though, and it's really hard for me to stop correcting her. She's so stupid sometimes."

The rest of the session was spent supporting the other teens in developing their humility skills—the part of making failures "mine."

Hey, Kids!

Kids, admitting you're wrong first when there's a problem is really hard, but when you do it there are a lot fewer problems. It takes a lot of strength to admit you're wrong and to control yourself to keep from doing the natural thing—blaming others. Remember, the Greeks knew all about it. They called it humility, *parus*, or "strength under control." Practice this stuff at home with your mom and dad.

So far we've seen how to make failures "mine." Now let's take a look at how to make successes "yours."

In this situation, watch how Adam not only admits his failure first but focuses only on the success of others (not mentioning once what the other person did wrong). This is Super-Bowl-level human behavior!

Adam's the editor of a school paper exclusively written and published by seniors. An article was published without Adam's review and it was full of errors. Within ten minutes of the paper being read by students and the principal, the intercom blared, "Adam McCurry, please come to the principal's office immediately."

Later that afternoon, at the Friday post-publishing wrap-up, Adam sat down with his staff. Most everyone was studying the pattern of the floor tile. His voice was solemn but steady as he tried to make eye contact with everyone. "Guys, I goofed up. I didn't do what I was supposed to do. I didn't review the final draft of the article in question. I'll do better next time. You all are so dedicated and work so hard. It's easy to skip steps. I just did. In our next Monday morning meeting, let's talk about some new procedures to safeguard against this happening again. Congratulations on the rest of the paper. It was great." They adjourned after some housekeeping issues were covered.

That's making failure "mine" and success "yours" in living color! Amazing. Are you wondering which hat I pulled that example from? Actually, it happens a lot in real life—and sometimes with older teens.

Here's a real-life adult example. Several years ago, author Jim Collins identified the two leadership qualities shared by the CEOs of the top eleven money-maker companies in the world in the late 1990s. Envelope, please: *Humility* and *strong will* (*Good to Great*, Collins 2001).

When Collins and his associates interviewed these eleven CEOs, they *could not* get them to brag about themselves, only about their employees. The leaders typically responded with something like "There are lots of people in this company who could do my job better than I do." Collins reports *every one* of these CEOs looked "out the window" toward employees when discussing success. But when it came to failures, all the CEOs switched their gazes to look "in the mirror" and blamed themselves.

So now we have a value-added quality of humility. It not only makes everyone feel good, it can also be a huge money maker!

Now we're ready to round out this chapter with our last rule for building humility in our children.

3. Make Others "Home"

Home is about comfort, about feeling at peace with *who I am* emotionally and physically. Our experience applying the Golden Rule has revealed that the deepest source of this home feeling is found in enduring healthy relationships, especially giving and taking with humility among family and friends.

I'll never forget the feeling of home I got from this memorable session several years ago.

Mel, a dad who had been divorced for four years, sat down for his first session and started by saying, "I know you wanted to interview me first, but I'd like to start with my two kids. I want them in here." Even after forty years of working on humility myself in my practice, I had to stifle my almost-blurted-out comments: "That's fine and dandy, but I need to talk with you alone first. That's the way an interview is done." I mustered the strength to zip it and managed to say, without a lot of enthusiasm, "Okay, let's have both kids come in right now."

And what a humility gift I got by witnessing this family in action.

Twelve-year-old Cara and ten-year-old Franklin sat on either side of their dad. Their glances at each other told the story about what a homey feeling family members had toward each other. They each looked at me, around the room, and back at dad, who smiled warmly and nodded supportively. Dad then clasped one hand of each child and, still smiling, focused on me and said, "We're having some anger problems and I'd like some help. I'm sure I'm not doing a lot of stuff right." He looked at both children warmly, squeezed their hands, and said to them as they smiled back at him, "I'd like for you to share your worries."

The rest of the session was about each child's sadness about two things: conflict with their mom, who lived in a nearby town, and some teasing that was going on at school. Franklin looked me straight in the eye and said, "I tried to tell Mom for the first time how her living in another town made me sad. She didn't say much, but she looked upset at me." Tears started coming down his cheeks. Dad handed him a tissue.

Franklin looked at his dad, who put his arm around his son's shoulder. Then Dad leaned forward and tried to make eye contact with Franklin. "It would be best if your mom could live here, but she can't get a job here. She's doing the best she can." That was just one of many humble statements—Dad pointing out positives about Mom instead of bad-mouthing her. Later I found out there was plenty of ammo in that "she's a bad mom" artillery box.

I went back to Franklin's sadness and said, "Franklin, you *should* be sad—and probably mad." He shook his head and grabbed more tissue to stop the tears. As we've mentioned multiple times, validating feelings is the best way to build self-assured children.

After discussing the ups and downs about their mom for ten minutes or so, Cara brought up how she was teased at school. After giving me the bullying details, she looked at me with the kindest eyes and said, "I feel so much with my heart. Can you help me not care so much?" She was only interested in correcting herself—looking into the mirror—not in blaming the bully. Was she just a weak kid? No, she was a child brimming with humility. Maybe she'll be the next leading CEO.

I asked Dad whether they had been in therapy as a family, and he looked out the window. Then he focused his smiling attention toward each child and turned back to me with this quiet comment: "No, we're just really close."

What a gift to see and feel the presence of such a comfortable home feeling through the sparkling warm colors of everyone's humility.

The Golden Rule. Can you think of any other rule that has such a profound impact in the healthy social and emotional development of a child? The depth of goodness one feels, both from being treated with humility and from treating others with humility, is unsurpassed. It underscores the truth and practical value of the apostle Paul's great advice in Philippians 2:3: "Do nothing out of selfish ambition or vain conceit, but in humility consider others better than yourselves."

Treat others as you want to be treated.

That's it. This part of our Golden Rule journey is completed. It's truly been a privilege to participate in some way in the parenting of your child. May we all continue to discover the unfolding richness of the Golden Rule. Your children are so fortunate to have such loving parents. May God bless you and your children.

CPSIA information can be obtained at www.ICGtesting.com
Printed in the USA
LVOW07s1710020815

448539LV00028B/991/P